Abortion – Rights and Ethics

ISSUES

Volume 171

Series Editor

Lisa Firth

Independence

Educational Publishers
Cambridge

First published by Independence
The Studio, High Green
Great Shelford
Cambridge CB22 5EG
England

© Independence 2009

British Library Cataloguing in Publication Data

Abortion: Rights and Ethics — (Issues; v. 171)
1. Abortion — moral and ethical aspects 2. Abortion
I. Series II. Firth, Lisa
363.4'6-dc22

ISBN-13: 978 1 86168 485 1

Printed in Great Britain

MWL Print Group Ltd

Cover

The illustration on the front cover is by
Simon Kneebone.

CONTENTS

Chapter One: Terminating a Pregnancy

Chapter Two: Abortion and Ethics

Useful information for readers

Dear Reader,

Issues: Abortion – Rights and Ethics

Abortion is a subject guaranteed to raise strong emotions and opinions. Statistics show that one in three women in the UK has an abortion before the age of 45. What are the ethical implications of this? Are there any health issues for a woman terminating her pregnancy? Should the legal time limit for an abortion be lowered? This title covers the ethical debate, legislation surrounding abortion and the medical procedures involved.

The purpose of *Issues*

Abortion – Rights and Ethics is the one hundred and seventy-first volume in the **Issues** series. The aim of this series is to offer up-to-date information about important issues in our world. Whether you are a regular reader or new to the series, we do hope you find this book a useful overview of the many and complex issues involved in the topic. This title replaces an older volume in the **Issues** series, Volume 126: **The Abortion Debate,** which is now out of print.

Titles in the **Issues** series are resource books designed to be of especial use to those undertaking project work or requiring an overview of facts, opinions and information on a particular subject, particularly as a prelude to undertaking their own research.

The information in this book is not from a single author, publication or organisation; the value of this unique series lies in the fact that it presents information from a wide variety of sources, including:

⇨ Government reports and statistics
⇨ Newspaper articles and features
⇨ Information from think-tanks and policy institutes
⇨ Magazine features and surveys
⇨ Website material
⇨ Literature from lobby groups and charitable organisations.*

Critical evaluation

Because the information reprinted here is from a number of different sources, readers should bear in mind the origin of the text and whether the source is likely to have a particular bias or agenda when presenting information (just as they would if undertaking their own research). It is hoped that, as you read about the many aspects of the issues explored in this book, you will critically evaluate the information presented. It is important that you decide whether you are being presented with facts or opinions. Does the writer give a biased or an unbiased report? If an opinion is being expressed, do you agree with the writer?

Abortion – Rights and Ethics offers a useful starting point for those who need convenient access to information about the many issues involved. However, it is only a starting point. Following each article is a URL to the relevant organisation's website, which you may wish to visit for further information.

Kind regards,

Lisa Firth
Editor, **Issues** series

* Please note that Independence Publishers has no political affiliations or opinions on the topics covered in the **Issues** *series, and any views quoted in this book are not necessarily those of the publisher or its staff.*

ISSUES TODAY
A RESOURCE FOR KEY STAGE 3

Younger readers can also now benefit from the thorough editorial process which characterises the **Issues** series with the launch of a new range of titles for 11- to 14-year-old students, **Issues Today**. In addition to containing information from a wide range of sources, rewritten with this age group in mind, **Issues Today** titles also feature comprehensive glossaries, an accessible and attractive layout and handy tasks and assignments which can be used in class, for homework or as a revision aid. In addition, these titles are fully photocopiable. For more information, please visit the **Issues Today** section of our website (www.independence.co.uk).

Having an abortion

Information provided by Best Health from the BMJ Publishing Group

This information tells you about an abortion to end a pregnancy. It explains the different types of abortion, how they work, what the risks are and what to expect afterwards.

The statistics we've included here are based on research studies. But some things, such as the chances of having complications, can vary from hospital to hospital. You may want to talk about this with the doctors and nurses treating you.

This information is about abortions for women who are less than 13 weeks pregnant. More than nine in ten women have their abortion in the first 13 weeks of pregnancy. However, in the UK, you can legally have an abortion at any time up to your 24th week of pregnancy.

What is an abortion?

An abortion is a way of ending your pregnancy. Abortions can be done with drugs or surgery.

⇨ Drugs cause your womb to cramp. The contents of your womb pass out of your vagina like a heavy period.
⇨ Surgery involves gently stretching the entrance to your womb (cervix) until it is wide enough for the fetus to be removed with a suction tube.

You can have either type of abortion at any stage of pregnancy, but it's safest to use drugs in very early pregnancy. Surgery isn't usually done before you are seven weeks pregnant. Before this, the fetus may be too small for the doctor to find.

You may not want to be pregnant because of circumstances at home or problems with your relationship. Your health may be at risk, or there may be a chance that the baby will have a medical problem. This information can't help you make the decision to have an abortion. What it does is to tell you what will happen if you decide to go ahead.

Whatever your reasons, no-one has to know about your abortion unless you want them to. Your usual doctor, partner or parents don't have to be informed, even if you are under 16. If you are under 16, most doctors will suggest you talk to your parents.

Can I have an abortion?

The law says you can have an abortion if:

⇨ you are less than 24 weeks pregnant;
⇨ two doctors agree that it would cause less damage to your physical or mental health than going on with the pregnancy. This is a legal requirement, but in many cases it is just a formality. You should be able to have an abortion if you choose to. If your usual doctor is unwilling to refer you for an abortion, you are entitled to go to another doctor who will. Charities which offer abortion advice, such as the British Pregnancy Advisory Service (http://www.bpas.org), can help with getting authorisation from two doctors.

You can only have an abortion after 24 weeks if there are exceptional circumstances, such as a risk to your health.

The doctor works out how many weeks pregnant you are by counting from the first day of your last period. The earlier in your pregnancy you have an abortion, the more likely it is to work and the safer it is.

Guidelines for doctors say that:

⇨ you shouldn't have to wait more than three weeks between asking for an abortion and your appointment;
⇨ you should be cared for separately from women who may be going ahead with a pregnancy;
⇨ you should be given the choice between an abortion using drugs or surgery. However, some hospitals don't offer both, so it's important

to check this with your doctor.

More than 190,000 women have an abortion in England and Wales each year. At least a third of British women will have had an abortion by the time they are 45.

There are more restrictions on abortion in Northern Ireland than there are in England, Wales and Scotland.

What happens during an abortion?

Preparing for an abortion

Before the abortion, your doctors will give you a check-up and ask about your health. You will have a blood test to make sure you have enough iron in your blood. You may have an ultrasound scan. This isn't essential, but it can tell you more precisely how many weeks pregnant you are.

If there's a risk that you have a sexually transmitted infection (STI), such as chlamydia, you may have tests to check. Having an STI can increase your risk of getting an infection after the abortion, so it's best to get it treated.

An abortion using drugs

An abortion using drugs is called a medical abortion. You might hear it called the abortion pill, but it doesn't just involve taking a pill. You need to take two different tablets, usually two days apart. You'll need to visit the clinic or hospital twice and have a check-up about a week later.

⇨ On the first visit you take tablets called mifepristone. These block the hormone that makes the lining of your womb hold onto the fetus. You should wait at the clinic for half an hour or so to make sure the tablets are working properly.

⇨ You can carry on as normal in the two days between appointments. You may get some bleeding or period-like pains.

⇨ On the second visit, about two days later, you'll be given one of two drugs. These are called misoprostol and gemeprost. They contain a hormone called prostaglandin, which makes your womb push out the fetus. They are usually given as a tablet that you put into your vagina. You can also get misoprostol tablets that you swallow, but it works better and has fewer side effects when used in your vagina.

⇨ You may be given a choice between going home and staying in the clinic or hospital after taking the second drug. You don't have to lie in bed. You may feel more comfortable walking around or watching television.

⇨ The drugs can sometimes make you feel sick, vomit or have diarrhoea. The cramps in your womb will be painful, but the nurse can give you a strong painkiller to help. The pain usually settles after the abortion.

The abortion usually happens after the second visit. It will be like a very heavy period with clots of blood. It should be over within four to six hours. You will keep bleeding after this, but it will be much lighter. You'll need to wear sanitary towels to soak up the blood as you may get an infection with tampons.

Occasionally, the abortion takes longer than four hours to start. If this happens, you may be given another dose of the second drug you took. Abortions can take longer to start in women who are more than nine weeks pregnant. You can be given up to four doses of the second drug, with a three-hour gap between doses, until the abortion happens.

It's important that you take the second drug, even though it means a second visit to the clinic. There is lots of research to show that taking two drugs works far better than taking one.

Drugs used for abortion

The second drug you take will be either misoprostol or gemeprost. Misoprostol was originally used for treating stomach ulcers. Many doctors use misoprostol for abortions, and studies show that it works and is safe. But it hasn't been licensed for abortions by the government organisation that decides on the safety of drugs. It's common for drugs to be used outside their original license, so there's no need to worry about this.

At least a third of British women will have had an abortion by the time they are 45

Having a surgical abortion

The operation doctors usually use for an abortion is called suction aspiration or vacuum aspiration. This is because the contents of your womb are gently sucked out with a tube and pump.

The operation takes about 10 minutes. You should expect to stay at the clinic for a few hours. You can usually go home the same day.

You don't have to get fully undressed. You'll be asked to take off your pants shortly beforehand.

The entrance to your womb may be softened with a hormone called prostaglandin. This is done to make it easier for your doctor to open your cervix without damaging it. You or your doctor may put a prostaglandin tablet into your vagina three hours before surgery. Or you may be given tablets to take at home a day or two before your operation.

You can have a general anaesthetic, which makes you sleep, or a local anaesthetic, which numbs the area around the entrance to your womb.

With a local anaesthetic you are awake and aware of what's happening, but you won't feel any pain. Your doctor or nurse will talk to you during surgery to make sure you're OK.

During a surgical abortion, the fetus is gently sucked out of your womb. The suction can be done with an electric pump or a syringe operated by hand. It doesn't involve any cutting. If you have an abortion using an electric pump, you will usually have a general anaesthetic.

Here's what happens.

⇨ First, the doctor inserts a small instrument called a speculum into your vagina so he or she can see your cervix. Your cervix is cleaned with a swab.

⇨ Your cervix is gently stretched and opened. A series of metal instruments called dilators are put into your cervix, starting with one that is two millimetres (one-twelfth of an inch) wide. Bigger ones are added until your cervix is open. How far open your cervix needs to be depends on how many weeks pregnant you are. If you are nine weeks pregnant, nine millimetres (a third of an inch) should be enough.

⇨ A thin plastic tube is put into your womb through the cervix. The contents of your womb are gently sucked into the tube using a pump.

⇨ If you're awake during surgery, you'll probably feel strong, period-type pains.

If you're having an abortion with a hand-held syringe, your cervix will not need to be opened beforehand, as the tube used is very thin and bendy. You will have a local anaesthetic and the abortion will probably happen in a small treatment room rather than an operating theatre. It takes longer than suction using an electric pump.

After a rest and a check-up, most women can leave the clinic within three hours. Driving isn't recommended for 48 hours after a general anaesthetic. You may be given antibiotics to prevent infection.

How well do abortions work?

Abortions usually work and most women are no longer pregnant afterwards. But there is a small chance that you will still be pregnant after your abortion.

⇨ Just over 2 in 1,000 women who have a surgical abortion are still pregnant afterwards.

⇨ Some studies show that as few as 2 in 1,000 women are still pregnant after a medical abortion. Other studies show that between 1 in 100 and 2 in 100 are still pregnant. The results of studies vary because they looked at different drugs.

Before the seventh week of pregnancy, a medical abortion works better than a surgical abortion.

Some women prefer surgery because they don't want the heavy blood loss you get after a medical abortion. Surgery is also quicker and happens in one go. Other women prefer to take drugs because they feel more in control, see it as more natural, or because they don't want the risks of surgery or an anaesthetic.

What if my abortion doesn't work?

An incomplete abortion means that part of the contents of your womb is left behind. This is more common with a medical abortion than a surgical one. You'll usually need surgery to remove the contents of your womb. About 2 in 100 women who have a medical abortion need surgery afterwards.

If your abortion hasn't worked at all, you may decide to have another or go ahead with the pregnancy. It's important to know that if you had a medical abortion and it didn't work, it's possible that one of the drugs could have harmed the fetus.

What are the risks of an abortion?

All medical procedures have risks. About 2 in 1,000 women who have an abortion get complications. But the earlier in pregnancy you have an abortion, the safer it is.

You are more likely to get problems in the two weeks after the abortion than at the time. Getting an infection is the biggest risk.

Problems at the time of the abortion

There is a risk of heavy bleeding (a haemorrhage) after an abortion. This happens to less than 2 in 1,000 women. About half of these women will need a blood transfusion. You are more likely to have heavy bleeding after a medical abortion.

Other risks of a medical abortion are:
⇨ pain, from cramps in your womb;
⇨ stomach problems, such as sickness and diarrhoea. These are caused by the drug prostaglandin;
⇨ fever and chills. These can be a side effect of prostaglandin. But they don't usually last very long.

If you have a surgical abortion, there's a higher risk of:
⇨ damage to your cervix. Some studies show this happens in up to 1 in 100 women who have a surgical abortion. Other studies show the risk is less than 1 in 1,000. The risk is lower for early abortions and if your surgeon is experienced;
⇨ damage to your womb. It's possible for surgery to tear your womb. This happens in around 1 in 1,000 to 4 in 1,000 abortions. Again, the risk is lower for early abortions and if your surgeon is experienced.

Problems within two weeks of the abortion

⇨ Up to one in ten women will get an infection after an abortion. An infection can lead to a more serious problem, called pelvic inflammatory disease. This needs to be treated quickly as it could stop you having a baby in the future. Taking antibiotics after your abortion reduces the risk of infection.
⇨ Your abortion might not get rid of all the contents of your womb. This can cause pain, bleeding or an infection. You may need surgery and a further course of antibiotics.

Longer-term problems

There's no evidence that having an abortion will harm your health or affect your chances of getting pregnant again. Most women who choose to can go on to have a healthy pregnancy.

You are no more likely to have problems with future pregnancies than a woman who hasn't had an abortion. Problems with pregnancy include the fetus growing outside your womb (an ectopic pregnancy) or the placenta covering the entrance to your womb (placenta praevia). There's no good evidence that having an abortion increases your risk of either of these problems.

Some research suggests that women who have an abortion and become pregnant again are more likely to have a miscarriage or a baby that's born too early. However, other studies show no link between abortions and miscarriages or premature births.

Having an abortion doesn't increase your risk of breast cancer. Some studies have suggested that there might be a link between abortions and breast cancer. But there's good-quality research to show this isn't true, and most experts say that having an abortion doesn't increase your risk. A recent study compared women who'd had an abortion with women who'd had a miscarriage. There was no increase in risk for women who'd had an abortion.

What other options are there?

Another type of surgery, called dilation and evacuation, is available, but it's usually only used for women who are more than 15 weeks pregnant. It uses a combination of electric suction and cutting with forceps. You usually need a general anaesthetic. Only 5 in 100 abortions in England and Wales use this method.

If you decide to go ahead with your pregnancy rather than having an abortion, there are still some choices available to you. You may decide to keep the baby. Or you may choose to have the baby looked after by foster parents or adopted.

For many women this is a very difficult decision. If you aren't sure about what to do, it may help to talk to someone. You may wish to contact the **fpa** on 0845 310 1334 or at www.fpa.org.uk

⇨ The above information is adapted and reproduced from an article originally published in Best Health from the BMJ Publishing Group and is reprinted with kind permission from the copyright holder. To view the original text and references, please visit the BMJ Group's Best Health website at http://besthealth.bmj.com

© BMJ Group

Recovering after an abortion

What happens to your body after an abortion and what are the warning signs to look out for if you've got an infection? TheSite.org looks at the physical and emotional symptoms you may experience

Go back to your doctor if you have:

⇨ Lasting or severe pain and cramps that don't subside, even with painkillers;

⇨ Discoloured or smelly discharge;

⇨ Abnormal tenderness of the breasts and sickness two weeks after the abortion;

⇨ Frequent passing of large clots;

⇨ A high temperature;

⇨ Continuous and heavy bleeding for more than two days afterwards.

Afterwards

You may feel scared and confused about how you're going to feel after an abortion. Even though at the time you may just want to get it over and done with, it's not always that easy to forget. 'All of the physical symptoms of pregnancy had gone, but after the abortion this was replaced by a different kind of pain,' said Amanda, who had an abortion at nine weeks. But for many women, they will recover quickly and deciding to stop the pregnancy was the right choice.

Bleeding

It's likely that you will experience some bleeding for about 14 days after the abortion and have pains similar to period pains. You may also feel sick and have spotting up to your next period. Don't worry if your periods take a while to settle down. 'I wasn't aware of the amount of bleeding I would have and how long I would be bleeding for afterwards,' says Amy, who had an abortion at 12 weeks. 'Also, how much it would mess up my cycle.'

'If you're soaking more than three sanitary towels per hour, or bleeding very heavily for a week, then you need to contact someone at the clinic or hospital,' says Lisa at Brook. 'Avoid using tampons to deal with the bleeding and use sanitary towels instead. There's no actual evidence to support that swimming will lead to infection, but it's probably best to avoid this for around two weeks afterwards to prevent that risk. It's also best to not have sex for two weeks.'

You should go back to your doctor (GP) around two to three weeks after the abortion to make sure that everything is OK. If you haven't done this already, this would be a good time to talk about what contraception is available to you to avoid another unwanted pregnancy. If there's anything you're worried about immediately after your abortion, speak to a nurse or make an appointment straight away. One of the most important things you can do is complete the course of antibiotics you're given to prevent against any infection.

Are there any risks?

⇨ There's no evidence to say that having an abortion, or more than one, will affect your fertility. There are risks associated with abortion, relating to which method you've had, and these will be explained to you by your doctor.

⇨ Infection is the most common risk of abortion and if that's not dealt with could lead to future problems with your fertility, in the same way that it could if you had an untreated STI.

⇨ A very small percentage of women will experience a missed abortion. Marie Stopes Centres, for example, say the risk is less than 1 in 10,000 abortions. If you are still experiencing pregnancy symptoms three weeks after your abortion, go back and see your doctor.

⇨ There is the possibility that a piece of tissue from the foetus may be left in the uterus. This can cause

ITS NOT OVER YET...

pain and may lead to infection, in which case a repeat procedure may be needed.

Post-abortion stress

Dealing with having an abortion can result in an array of emotions, including sleeping problems, a sense of loss and emptiness and depression. If you are feeling low, or it's affecting your relationships and general wellbeing, it's important you speak to someone you can confide in. 'Certain physical things shocked me about having an abortion,' says Amy. 'I remember coming round afterwards and wondering what I was doing there and what had happened. The hardest thing for me to grasp was that I went in with a baby that had been in me for 12 weeks and came out of the same room without a baby in me. How could my baby have gone, just like that, in a matter of minutes? I didn't get to say goodbye and I wasn't prepared with how to get to grips with it afterwards.'

You should be offered a free counselling session after an abortion. Some of the larger service providers will let you take up this session up to a year after the procedure. You can also go to independent counsellors, your doctor or nurse, and they can refer you for counselling on the NHS. 'Most women don't experience serious feelings of regret or grief after an abortion,' says Rebecca at **fpa**. 'When they do it's normally about the situation of how the abortion took place; perhaps they wanted to carry on with the pregnancy and they couldn't because of personal situations. The important thing is not to suffer in silence and to ask for help if you need it. Some counselling services are run and financed by groups that oppose abortion and their aim is to stop you from having an abortion. If you feel that something isn't right about the information that you are receiving then think about going somewhere else for advice.'
Written by Julia Pearlman

⇨ The above information is reprinted with kind permission from TheSite. Visit www.thesite.org for more information.
© *TheSite*

History of legal abortion

Information from Life

1861 – The Offences Against the Person act
Sections 58 and 59 outlaw abortion and made it a criminal offence, punishable by imprisonment, to assist in attempting an unlawful abortion by any means whatsoever.

1929 – The Infant Life (Preservation) Act
The crime of child destruction filled a gap in the law and protected babies in the course of being born. This act made it illegal to kill a child 'capable of being born alive'. If the pregnancy had lasted more than 28 weeks the child was presumed to be viable and was therefore protected. The act was specifically left unaffected by the Abortion Act 1967, but has virtually been set aside by the 1990 Act.

1967 – The Abortion Act
This does not give a woman the right to an abortion but protects a doctor who performs one from being prosecuted – if two doctors certify that in their opinion, formed in good faith, an abortion should be carried out. The grounds for legal abortion are:
1 Risk to the life of the mother;
2 To prevent grave permanent injury to the physical or mental health of the mother;
3 Risk of injury to the physical or mental health of the mother greater than if the pregnancy were terminated;
4 Risk of injury to the physical or mental health of existing (i.e. born) children;
5 Substantial risk of the children being born seriously handicapped;
6 In an emergency – to save the mothers life;
7 In an emergency – to prevent grave permanent injury to the physical or mental health of the mother.

1990 – Human Fertilisation and Embryology Act (HFE Act 1990)
Section 37 of the HFE Act amended the 1967 Abortion Act by reducing the time limit for abortions to 24 weeks when performed on grounds C and D of the Abortion Act. The time limit was removed for abortions performed on any other ground, enabling them to be carried out up to birth.

⇨ The above information is reprinted with kind permission from Life. Visit www.lifecharity.org.uk for more information.
© *Life*

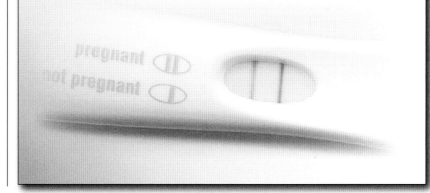

History of abortion law in the UK

Information from Abortion Rights

The first references to abortion in English law appeared in the 13th Century. The law followed Church teaching that abortion was acceptable until 'quickening', which, it was believed, was when the soul entered the fetus. The legal situation remained like this for centuries.

⇨ 1803: The Ellenborough Act – abortion after 'quickening' (i.e. when movement is felt at 16-20 weeks) carried the death penalty. Previously the punishment had been less severe.

⇨ 1837: The Ellenborough Act was amended to remove the distinction between abortion before and after quickening.

⇨ 1861: The Offences Against the Person Act – performing an abortion or trying to self-abort carried a sentence of life imprisonment.

⇨ 1929: Infant Life Preservation Act – this created a new crime of killing a viable fetus (at that time fixed at 28 weeks) in all cases except when the woman's life was at risk. However, it was not clear whether it would be legal to terminate for the same reason before 28 weeks.

In the 19th century and early part of the 20th century, a succession of laws were brought in to reduce access to legal abortion. These laws effectively controlled women's lives until 1967. But they did not, of course, prevent unwanted pregnancy, or the need for abortion. Thousands of women resorted to back-street abortionists, permanently damaging their health or dying. Newspapers advertised cures for 'menstrual blockages', but women knew they were abortifacients. Many of these were ineffective and were also poisonous; one of the cheapest, a lead-based potion, poisoned and blinded many women.

⇨ 1923-33: 15 per cent of maternal deaths were due to illegal abortion.

'In the thirties, my aunt died self-aborting. She had three children and couldn't feed a fourth ... So she used a knitting needle. She died of septicaemia, leaving her children motherless.'

'A high percentage of maternal mortality is due to attempted abortion ..... We, as a House of Commons and as a nation, must face up to that fact today.'

During the 1930s, women's groups and MPs were deeply concerned about the great loss of life and damage to health resulting from unsafe, illegal abortion. The Conference of Co-operative Women was the first organisation to pass a resolution (1934) calling for the legalisation of abortion. The Abortion Law Reform Association was established in 1936.

⇨ 1936: The Abortion Law Reform Association (ALRA) was established; its aim was to campaign for the legalisation of abortion.

⇨ 1938: Dr Alex Bourne was acquitted of having performed an illegal abortion. This set a case-law precedent.

Two years later, in a landmark case, Dr Alex Bourne was acquitted of having performed an illegal abortion. He believed that abortion should be legal in exceptional circumstances and, most courageously, admitted having performed an abortion for a gang-raped 14-year-old who was suicidal. He argued that the law did permit abortion before 28 weeks and did allow abortion when a woman's mental or physical health was in danger. The court agreed that this was a life-threatening situation and acquitted Dr Bourne. As a result some

women were able to get a safe abortion. However, uncertainty remained as a psychiatrist's approval was needed. It was usually only educated and/or relatively wealthy women who had the resources to find, and pay for, a compliant psychiatrist.

In 1939, the Birkett Committee was set up by the government to clarify whether doctors could perform an abortion to save a woman's life, but their work was interrupted by the outbreak of World War II.

⇨ 1939: The Birkett Committee, which had been set up by the Government in 1936, recommended clarification that doctors could perform an abortion to save a woman's life. Unfortunately World War II interrupted any implementation of its findings.

⇨ 1952-61: ALRA campaigned unsuccessfully for bills to legalise abortion. Support for reform grew.

In the fifties, support for reform grew. During the 1960s, fertility control became more widespread with the growth of the women's movement and availability of the contraceptive pill. However, illegal abortion was still killing or ruining the health of many women. ALRA led the campaign in support of David Steel MP's private member's bill to legalise abortion.

⇨ 1967: The Abortion Act (sponsored by David Steel, MP) became law, legalising abortion under certain conditions; it came into effect on 27 April 1968.

Since its passage in 1967 the Abortion Act has been unsuccessfully challenged several times by anti-choice ('pro-life') organisations which aim to restrict access to abortion.

In 1974, the Abortion Act was threatened by James White's private member's bill, sponsored by an anti-choice organisation. ALRA and other pro-choice groups combined to defend the 1967 Act against this and successive attacks. Whilst ALRA and others made more formal representations, women's groups organised demonstrations and meetings, many brandishing wire coat-hangers, symbolic of dangerous back-street abortion methods. The campaign led to the formation of the National Abortion Campaign (NAC) in 1975. The first meeting was held in the House of Commons on 10 March.

⇨ 1975: The National Abortion Campaign (NAC) was established to protect the 1967 Act and campaign for its improvement.
⇨ 1990: The Human Fertilisation and Embryology Bill introduced specific time-limits on abortion; it came into effect on 1 April 1991.

In 1990, the Human Fertilisation and Embryology Act introduced controls over new techniques which had been developed to help infertile couples and to monitor experiments on embryos. Despite attempts to use this law to restrict abortion rights, the 1990 Act lowered the legal time limit from 28 to 24 weeks, which is the currently accepted point of viability. It also clarified the circumstances under which abortion could be obtained at a later stage.

⇨ 2003: NAC and ALRA merged to form Abortion Rights.

⇨ The above information is reprinted with kind permission from Abortion Rights. Visit their website at www.abortionrights.org.uk for more information on this and other related topics.

© Abortion Rights

Abortion statistics

Statistics taken from the Department of Health statistical bulletin 'Abortion statistics, England and Wales: 2007'.

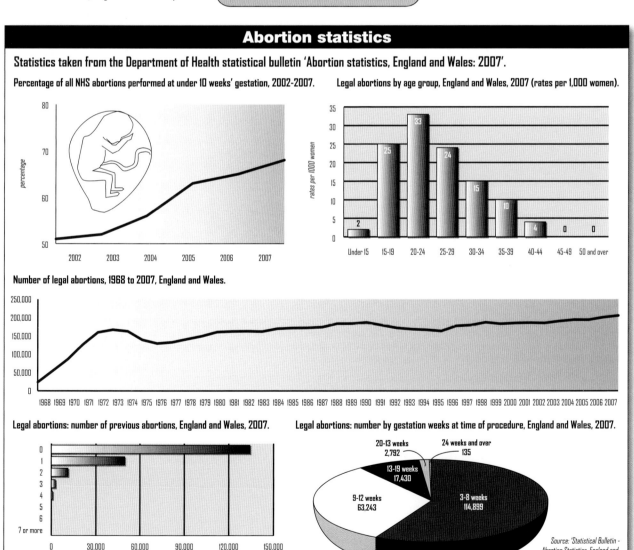

Percentage of all NHS abortions performed at under 10 weeks' gestation, 2002-2007.

Legal abortions by age group, England and Wales, 2007 (rates per 1,000 women).

Number of legal abortions, 1968 to 2007, England and Wales.

Legal abortions: number of previous abortions, England and Wales, 2007.

Legal abortions: number by gestation weeks at time of procedure, England and Wales, 2007.

20-13 weeks 2,792
24 weeks and over 135
13-19 weeks 17,430
9-12 weeks 63,243
3-8 weeks 114,899

Source: 'Statistical Bulletin - Abortion Statistics, England and Wales: 2007', published June 2008 by the Department of Health. Crown copyright.

Attitudes towards abortion – survey

Conducted by Ipsos MORI on behalf of Marie Stopes International

In total, 19% of all respondents disagree that, in general, all women should have the right of access to an abortion, 57% agree and 24% are neutral, do not know or prefer not to answer.

When presented with a list of potential circumstances (see question below), six out of ten (61%) British women aged 18-49 say there are certain circumstances in which they think a woman should have the right to access an abortion between 20 and 24 weeks.

3% say that a woman should not be able to access an abortion between 20 and 24 weeks, regardless of her circumstances, and a further 19% were not asked this question as they disagree with abortion in general, giving a total of 22%.

4% of respondents both support a woman's right of access to an abortion yet also feel there are no grounds for abortion between 20 and 24 weeks.

Technical details
⇨ The Ipsos MORI Social Research Institute carried out face-to-face interviews with a representative quota sample of 1,032 women aged 18-49 across Great Britain between 2 and 15 May 2008.
⇨ The questions were 'self-completed' by respondents.
⇨ All data have been weighted to the known profile of the GB population.
20 May 2008

⇨ The above information is reprinted with kind permission from Ipsos MORI. Visit www.ipsos-mori. com for more information.
© *Ipsos MORI*

Public opinion on access to abortion

Statistics taken from Ipsos MORI's 'Attitudes Towards Abortion Survey'.

Respondents were asked: 'In general, to what extent do you agree or disagree that all women should have the right to access an abortion? Please select one option only.'

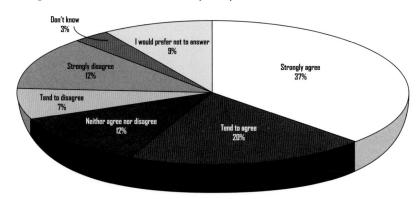

Don't know 3%
I would prefer not to answer 9%
Strongly disagree 12%
Tend to disagree 7%
Neither agree nor disagree 12%
Tend to agree 20%
Strongly agree 37%

Respondents were asked: 'Abortion is currently legal within 24 weeks. That is, a woman is allowed to have an abortion at any time within the first 24 weeks of her pregnancy, when two doctors have agreed that the abortion is in the interests of her physical or mental health. A very small proportion of abortions (fewer than 2 in 100) take place between 20 and 24 weeks. There is currently a debate about the legal time limit. In which, if any, of the following circumstances do you think a woman should have the right to access an abortion between 20 and 24 weeks? You may select more than one option.'

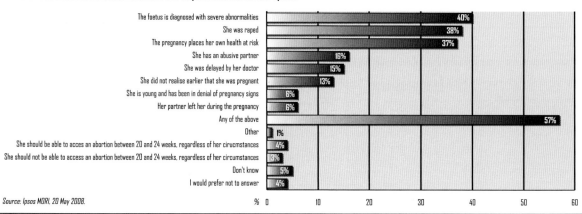

Circumstance	%
The foetus is diagnosed with severe abnormalities	40%
She was raped	38%
The pregnancy places her own health at risk	37%
She has an abusive partner	16%
She was delayed by her doctor	15%
She did not realise earlier that she was pregnant	13%
She is young and has been in denial of pregnancy signs	6%
Her partner left her during the pregnancy	6%
Any of the above	57%
Other	1%
She should be able to acces an abortion between 20 and 24 weeks, regardless of her cirucmstances	4%
She should not be able to access an abortion between 20 and 24 weeks, regardless of her circumstances	3%
Don't know	5%
I would prefer not to answer	4%

Source: Ipsos MORI, 20 May 2008.

Abortions linked to mental illness

Women who have an abortion are 30 per cent more likely to develop a mental illness, some research suggests

They are also three times more likely to develop a drug or alcohol addiction compared with other women, another report claimed.

Anxiety and drug abuse are the most common mental problems following an abortion

It comes as the number of women having an abortion in England and Wales exceeded 200,000 for the first time last year.

More abortions – 57,000 – were carried out on women aged 20 to 24 than any other age group. There were 4,400 on the under-16s.

A study of 500 women published in the British Journal of Psychiatry showed that anxiety and drug abuse are the most common mental problems following an abortion.

By Ben Leach

Professor David Fergusson, who led the research, said the findings had 'important implications' – because more than 90 per cent of British abortions were authorised on the grounds that keeping an unwanted baby would cause the mother mental health problems.

He said: 'There is nothing in this study that would suggest that the termination of pregnancy was associated with lower risks of mental health problems than birth.'

A second study shows that women who lose a baby by the age of 21 – either through an abortion or a miscarriage – are three times more likely to develop a drug or alcohol problem than others.

Researcher Kaeleen Dingle, of the University of Queensland, Australia, said: 'Abortion and miscarriage are stressful life events that have been shown to lead to anxiety, sadness and grief and, for some women, serious

depression and substance use disorders.'

Ann Furedi of the British Pregnancy Advisory Service admitted abortion could cause a huge amount of stress and anxiety, but added: 'Abortion does not necessarily cause the problem. It can be linked to other events in their life.'

30 November 2008

© *Telegraph Group Limited, London 2008*

Abortion 'does not cause mental health problems'

Major study from influential American body finds abortion does not cause women to have mental health problems

The American Psychological Association has issued findings from a comprehensive two-year review of published research on abortion and mental health. The APA concluded that there is 'no credible evidence that a single elective abortion of an unwanted pregnancy in and of itself causes mental health problems for adult women'.

The APA evaluated studies in peer-reviewed journals since 1989. They found that some studies indicate that some women experience sadness, grief and feelings of loss following an abortion, and some may experience 'clinically significant disorders, including depression and anxiety.' However, the task force found 'no evidence sufficient to support the

claim that an observed association between abortion history and mental health was caused by the abortion *per se*, as opposed to other factors.'

The report noted that other co-occurring risk factors, including poverty, prior exposure to violence, a history of emotional problems, a history of drug or alcohol use and prior unwanted births predispose women to experience both unwanted pregnancies and mental health problems after a pregnancy, irrespective of how the pregnancy is resolved.

According to the report, women terminating a wanted pregnancy, who perceived pressure from others to terminate their pregnancy, or who perceived a need to keep their abortion secret from their family and friends because of stigma associated with abortion, were more likely to experience negative psychological reactions following abortion.

The task force's conclusions are consistent with the conclusions of a similar APA review published prior to 1989. Results of that review were published in *Science* in 1990 and in the *American Psychologist* in 1992. A full copy of the task force's report may be accessed at http://www.apa.org/releases/abortion-report.pdf

Ann Furedi, Chief Executive of the family planning charity BPAS, which provided 55,000 abortions in 2007, said of this important literature review:

'The long-term psychological effects of abortion have been studied repeatedly since the legalisation of abortion in Britain and the United States. Abortion research is highly politicised but large, high-quality studies consistently show that having an abortion does not result in psychological damage.

'Psychological research is often cited by groups who oppose the availability of legal abortion. Abortion disrupts their view of the "natural" role of women as childbearers and mothers, so these groups strongly believe that abortion can only impact detrimentally on women's psychological wellbeing. But far from being a traumatic aberration, abortion is among the commonest medical interventions that women have.

'No woman ever wants to need an abortion, but for many, it is the solution to the very serious problem of an unintended pregnancy which they feel completely unable to cope with'

'One in three women in the UK has an abortion before the age of 45. There has not been a mass epidemic of abortion-induced mental illness resulting from this. No woman ever wants to need an abortion, but for many, it is the solution to the very serious problem of an unintended pregnancy which they feel completely unable to cope with.'

Notes

One in three women have an abortion before the age of 45 in the UK. See the Royal College of Obstetricians and Gynaecologist's evidence-based guidance from 2004, 'The care of women requesting induced abortion', p1. http://www.rcog.org.uk/index.asp?PageID=662

A woman faced with an unintended pregnancy must decide to either to continue the pregnancy and bring up the child, or to have an abortion, or to put the baby up for adoption. These are serious and necessarily time-limited decisions. For some women, talking things through with a supportive, neutral person who is able to offer information on all three options can be helpful in allowing them to reach their own decision.

In recognition of this, the Department of Health registers and approves organisations offering counselling and referring women for abortion as Pregnancy Advice Bureaux, if they comply with their Required Standard Operating Principles.[i] These require the monitoring of the counselling information on all pregnancy options for 'availability, clarity, content, balance and tone' as part of a regulatory framework which also includes unannounced inspection by Department of Health officials.

[i] 'Procedures For The Registration Of Pregnancy Advice Bureaux', Department of Health, 2001. http://www.dh.gov.uk/en/Publicationsandstatistics/Publications/PublicationsPolicyAndGuidance/DH_4005566

17 August 2008

⇨ The above information is reprinted with kind permission from *Abortion Review*, a professional journal produced by the British Pregnancy Advisory Service (BPAS). Visit www.bpas.org for more information.

© *British Pregnancy Advisory Service (BPAS)*

Facts on induced abortion worldwide

Information from the Guttmacher Institute

Worldwide incidence and trends

⇨ The number of induced abortions declined worldwide between 1995 and 2003, from nearly 46 million to approximately 42 million. About one in five pregnancies worldwide ends in abortion.

⇨ For every 1,000 women of child-bearing age (15-44) worldwide, 29 were estimated to have had an induced abortion in 2003, compared with 35 in 1995.

⇨ The decline in abortion incidence was greater in developed countries, where nearly all abortions are safe and legal (from 39 to 26 abortions per 1,000 women aged 15-44), than in developing countries, where more than half are unsafe and illegal (from 34 to 29).

⇨ Most abortions occur in developing countries – 35 million annually, compared with seven million in developed countries – a disparity that largely reflects the relative population distribution.

⇨ On the other hand, a woman's likelihood of having an abortion is similar whether she lives in a developed or developing region; in 2003, there were 26 abortions per 1,000 women aged 15-44 in developed countries compared with 29 per 1,000 in developing countries.

Regional incidence and trends

⇨ The most dramatic decline in abortion incidence occurred in Eastern Europe, a region where abortion is, for the most part, legal and safe: the rate fell from 90 to 44. The decrease coincided with substantial increases in contraceptive use in the region.

⇨ Although abortion rates and ratios (the number of abortions for every 100 births) in Eastern Europe have fallen significantly in recent years, they remain higher than in any other region. In 2003, there were more abortions than births in that region (105 abortions for every 100 births).

⇨ The estimated number of induced abortions in Africa has increased since 1995; however, the region's abortion rate has declined because of an increase in the number of reproductive-age women.

⇨ Induced abortion rates and numbers in Asia and Latin America show modest declines since 1995.

⇨ The lowest abortion rate in the world is in Western Europe (12 per 1,000 women aged 15-44).

The rate is 17 in Northern Europe and 21 in Northern America (Canada and the United States of America).

⇨ Because the world's population is concentrated in Asia, most abortions occur there (26 million yearly); nine million of these take place in China.

Worldwide, an estimated five million women are hospitalised each year for treatment of abortion-related complications

---

Abortion law

⇨ Legal restrictions on abortion do not affect its incidence. For example, the abortion rate is 29 in Africa, where abortion is illegal in many circumstances in most countries, and it is 28 in Europe, where abortion is generally permitted on broad grounds. The lowest rates in the world are in Western and Northern Europe, where abortion is accessible with few restrictions.

⇨ Where abortion is legal and permitted on broad grounds, it is generally safe, and where it is illegal in many circumstances, it is often unsafe. For example, in South Africa, the incidence of infection resulting from abortion decreased by 52% after the abortion law was liberalised in 1996.

⇨ Between 1995 and 2005, 17 countries liberalised their laws to increase access to safe abortion: Albania, Benin, Bhutan, Burkina Faso, Cambodia, Chad, Colombia, Ethiopia, Guinea,

Abortion worldwide: incidence and rates

Global and regional estimates of induced abortion, 1995 and 2003.

Region and subregion	No. of abortions (millions)		Abortion rate*	
	1995	2003	1995	2003
World	45.6	41.6	35	29
Developed countries	10.0	6.6	39	26
Excluding Eastern Europe	3.8	3.5	20	19
Developing countries**	35.5	35.0	34	29
Excluding China	24.9	26.4	33	30
Estimates by region				
Africa	5.0	5.6	33	29
Asia	26.8	25.9	33	29
Europe	7.7	4.3	48	28
Latin America	4.2	4.1	37	31
Northern America	1.5	1.5	22	21
Oceania	0.1	0.1	21	17

* Abortions per 1,000 women aged 15-44.   ** Those within Africa, the Americas excluding Canada and the USA, Asia excluding Japan, and Oceania excluding Australia and New Zealand.

Source: Guttmacher Institute, Facts on induced abortion worldwide, In Brief.

Mali, Nepal, Portugal, Saint Lucia, South Africa, Swaziland, Switzerland and Togo. Three countries tightened restrictions on abortion: El Salvador, Nicaragua and Poland.

Unsafe abortion

⇨ The World Health Organisation defines unsafe abortion as a procedure for terminating an unintended pregnancy carried out either by persons lacking the necessary skills or in an environment that does not conform to minimal medical standards, or both.

⇨ Worldwide, 48% of all induced abortions are unsafe. However, in developed regions, nearly all abortions (92%) are safe, whereas in developing countries, more than half (55%) are unsafe.

⇨ More than 95% of abortions in Africa and Latin America are performed under unsafe circumstances, as are about 60% of abortions in Asia (excluding Eastern Asia).

⇨ The worldwide unsafe abortion rate was essentially unchanged between 1995 and 2003 (15 and 14 abortions per 1,000 women aged 15-44, respectively). Because the overall abortion rate declined during this period, the proportion of all abortions that are unsafe increased from 44% to 47%.

Consequences of unsafe abortion

⇨ Worldwide, an estimated five million women are hospitalised each year for treatment of abortion-related complications such as haemorrhage and sepsis.

⇨ Complications due to unsafe abortion procedures account for an estimated 13% of maternal deaths worldwide, or 67,000 per year.

⇨ Almost all abortion-related deaths occur in developing countries. They are highest in Africa, where there were an estimated 650 deaths per 100,000 unsafe abortions in 2003, compared with 10 per 100,000 in developed regions.

⇨ Approximately 220,000 children worldwide lose their mothers

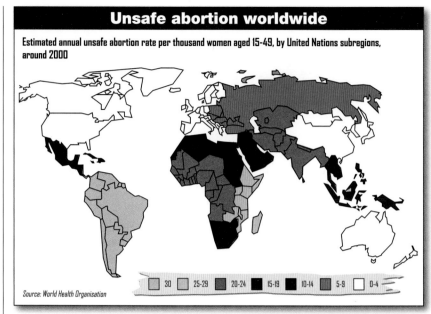

Unsafe abortion worldwide

Estimated annual unsafe abortion rate per thousand women aged 15-49, by United Nations subregions, around 2000

Source: World Health Organisation

Legend: 30 | 25-29 | 20-24 | 15-19 | 10-14 | 5-9 | 0-4

every year from abortion-related deaths.

⇨ Additional consequences of unsafe abortion include loss of productivity, economic burden on public health systems, stigma and long-term health problems such as infertility.

Unintended pregnancies: the root of abortion

⇨ More than one-third of the approximately 205 million pregnancies that occur worldwide annually are unintended, and about 20% of all pregnancies end in induced abortion.

⇨ Of the 23 million pregnancies that occur in developed countries, more than 40% are unintended, and 28% end in induced abortion.

⇨ Of the 182 million pregnancies that occur in developing countries, more than one-third are unintended, and 19% end in induced abortion (8% are safe procedures and 11% are unsafe).

⇨ The average woman must use some form of effective contraception for at least 20 years if she wants to limit her family size to two children, and 16 years if she wants four children.

⇨ Two-thirds of unintended pregnancies in developing countries occur among women who are not using any method of contraception.

⇨ More than 100 million married women in developing countries have an unmet need for con-

traception, meaning they are sexually active; are able to become pregnant; do not want to have a child soon or at all; and are not using any method of contraception, either modern or traditional.

⇨ The reasons why women (married and unmarried) do not use contraceptives most commonly include concerns about possible health and side-effects and the belief that they are not at risk of getting pregnant.

Samples of unsafe abortion methods used

⇨ Drinking turpentine, bleach or tea made with livestock manure.

⇨ Inserting herbal preparations into the vagina or cervix.

⇨ Placing foreign bodies, such as a stick, coat hanger or chicken bone, into the uterus.

⇨ Jumping from the top of stairs or a roof.

Most data in this fact sheet are from research conducted by the Guttmacher Institute and the World Health Organisation. Additional sources are notes in the fully annotated version, available at www.guttmacher.org and at www.who.int/reproductive-health
October 2008

⇨ Guttmacher Institute, 'Facts on induced abortion worldwide', *In Brief*, New York: Guttmacher Institute, 2008, http://www.guttmacher.org/pubs/fb_IAW.html, accessed 7 April 2009.

© Guttmacher Institute

Obama lifts funds ban for overseas abortion

Information from the Christian Institute

In one of his first acts as President, Barack Obama has lifted a ban on federal funding for international abortion groups.

The move means that US taxpayers will be funding one side of a political issue which is perhaps the most hotly contested in American politics: abortion.

He signed the executive order late on Friday but did not invite the media to cover the event.

Pro-life groups will interpret the decision to lift the ban as provocative and it is likely to open deep rifts in American politics.

British commentator, Melanie Phillips, said: 'Abortion is possibly the most toxic and divisive issue in American politics.

'Obama has said he wants to end the "culture wars" in America; it is hard to think of a more effective way of igniting them,' she added.

A number of commentators have noted that the President's inauguration speech glaringly omitted 'the right to life' when talking about the nation's founding principles.

During the speech the President noted the 'noble idea, passed on from generation to generation: the God-given promise that all are equal, all are free and all deserve a chance to pursue their full measure of happiness.'

But the Declaration of Independence famously asserts the right to 'Life, Liberty and the pursuit of Happiness'.

The Planned Parenthood Federation of America is the nation's largest provider of abortion services. It hailed President Obama for 'lifting the stranglehold on women's health across the globe with the stroke of a pen.'

'No longer will health care providers be forced to choose between receiving family planning funding and restricting the health care services they provide to women,' the organisation said in a statement.

But pro-life groups have criticised the move. Douglas Johnson, legislative director of the National Right to Life Committee, said it would guarantee more abortions.

He said: 'President Obama not long ago told the American people that he would support policies to reduce abortions, but today he is effectively guaranteeing more abortions by funding groups that promote abortion as a method of population control.'

According to news reports, President Obama is also expected to restore funding to the UN Population Fund (UNFPA) in the next budget.

The previous administration under President George W. Bush said the fund's work in China supported a Chinese family planning policy of coercive abortion and involuntary sterilisation. But the UNFPA has vehemently denied those claims.

The current White House agenda states that President Obama has pledged to oppose any constitutional amendment to protect the lives of unborn children.

He says he will actively defend Roe v. Wade, a legal ruling which effectively legalised abortion in America.

He also plans to overturn a ban on embryonic stem cell research which involves the destruction of human embryos. This comes at a time when ethical alternatives are proving more successful.

27 January 2009

⇨ The above information is reprinted with kind permission from the Christian Institute. Visit www. christian.org.uk for more.

© *Christian Institute*

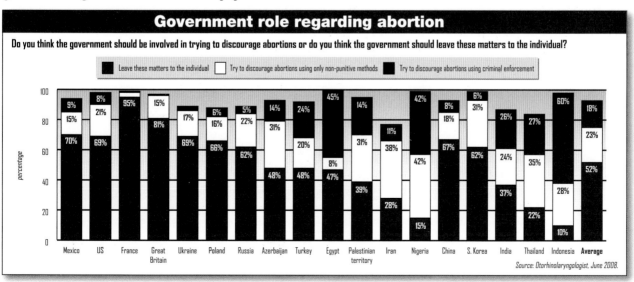

Government role regarding abortion

Do you think the government should be involved in trying to discourage abortions or do you think the government should leave these matters to the individual?

■ Leave these matters to the individual   ☐ Try to discourage abortions using only non-punitive methods   ■ Try to discourage abortions using criminal enforcement

Source: Otorhinolaryngologist. June 2008.

'Global Gag Rule' rescinded

Evidence replaces ideology as President Obama reverses 'disastrous' Bush policy

Today, 23 January 2009, President Barack Obama rescinded the Global Gag Rule, one of the most controversial and ideologically-motivated policies imposed by former President Bush.

The Global Gag Rule, re-imposed in 2001, stated that U.S. funding for family planning was denied to any non-U.S. non-governmental organisations (NGOs) that used their own money to:

⇨ provide counselling and referral for abortion, even in countries where abortion is legal

⇨ advocate to make abortion legal or more available in their country, even at the request of their own government

⇨ perform abortions in cases other than a threat to the life of the woman, rape or incest.

However, anti-abortion advocacy was allowed, underscoring the ideological nature of the Gag Rule.

Dr. Gill Greer, Director General of the International Planned Parenthood Federation, said:

'For eight long years the Global Gag Rule has been used by the Bush administration to play politics with the lives of poor women across the world.

'In rescinding this disastrous and unjust policy, President Obama has returned the United States to the international consensus on women's health and begun the process of repairing the damage of the last eight years.

'IPPF estimates that during the Bush administration it lost at least US$100 million for the life-saving family planning and sexual and reproductive health services that our grassroots national affiliates in over 100 developing countries deliver to their communities.

'Based on internationally-recognised estimates, this funding would have prevented 36 million unintended pregnancies and 15 million induced abortions.

'More tragically, 80,000 women's and 2.5 million infants' and children's lives would have been saved. This is the true legacy of the Global Gag Rule.'

The Gag Rule, and the dangerous ideology that supports it, puts non-governmental organisations from outside the United States in an untenable position, forcing them to choose between carrying out their work to improve the health and rights of women or lose their funding from the United States.

It would have imposed unethical, unsafe restrictions upon IPPF medical practitioners by requiring them to deny medically-necessary information to their clients, and so violate the trust of their communities.

This 'gag' is an attack upon freedom of speech that, if attempted in the United States, would be ruled unconstitutional.

The Gag Rule has had a devastating impact upon the breadth and effectiveness of the delivery of family planning, sexual health and contraceptive services around the world, particularly in Africa where only 18 per cent of women have access to modern contraception, compared to 56 per cent in the rest of the developing world.

The de-funding of IPPF and others has directly contributed to this.

When the Planned Parenthood Association of Ghana, an African pioneer in sexual and reproductive health, lost U.S. funding for its rural outreach programmes, condom distribution fell by 40 per cent overnight, impacting family planning and HIV prevention programmes.

In addition, 38,000 women who had regularly been receiving contraceptive supplies from PPAG were no longer able to obtain them, and an additional 20,000 women and children could no longer access maternal and child health services.

In 2009 it still has not been possible to replace the distribution network PPAG had developed in rural Ghana prior to the Gag Rule and instances of unsafe abortion have risen by up to 50 per cent in some areas.

Dr. Greer continued:

'The Gag Rule has done immense harm and caused untold suffering to millions around the world; it has undermined health systems and endangered the lives and health of the poorest and most vulnerable women on the planet by denying access to life-saving family planning, sexual and reproductive health and HIV services and exposing them to the dangers of unsafe abortion.

'More insidiously, it formed the basis for a concerted attack by the Bush administration upon reproductive rights that saw discussion, even of family planning, stifled at the international level and gains in women's health and rights reversed.

'IPPF celebrates the commitment by President Obama to discard policies harmful to women and looks forward to working with the Obama administration to open a new chapter in women's health.'

In 2001 when the Gag Rule was re-imposed, the European Commission and donor governments recognised the devastating impact it would have upon health provision around the world and increased funding to cover some, but not all, of the lost funding from the U.S.

The result was that clinics closed, medical staff were lost and family planning, sexual and reproductive health and HIV services were cut back, affecting many communities in developing countries.
23 January 2009

⇨ The above information is reprinted with kind permission from the International Planned Parenthood Federation. Visit www.ippf.org for more information.

Northern Ireland clarifies when abortion is legal

Information from the *Irish Times*

**By Gerry Moriarty,
Northern Editor**

The Department of Health in Northern Ireland has produced guidelines aimed at providing clarity on when abortion can be permitted in the North.

Pro-choice groups have welcomed the move while some anti-abortion representatives have characterised the guidelines as an attempt to legalise abortion through the 'back door'.

> **'The guidelines recognise and reaffirm the present legal situation – that, except where it is required to preserve the life of the woman, abortion is illegal in Northern Ireland'**

The guidelines were issued on the back of a Court of Appeal judgment five years ago calling on the department to provide clarity on abortion in Northern Ireland.

The guidelines were approved by the Northern Executive, although DUP Ministers on the Executive opposed the guidelines. Sinn Féin, the Ulster Unionist Party and the SDLP supported the proposals.

The guidelines make no changes to the law in Northern Ireland and do not extend the British 1967 Abortion Act to the North.

The Department of Health outlines that in summary abortion is legal where 'it is necessary to preserve the life of the woman or there is a risk of real and serious adverse effect on her physical or mental health, which is either long term or permanent'.

'In any other circumstances it would be unlawful to perform such an operation,' its guidelines add.

Foetal abnormality is not recognised as a ground for abortion in itself, although if it was found to constitute a serious threat to the physical or mental health of the woman it would. There is no reference to rape in the guidelines, although again abortion would be permitted if it were found to constitute a serious physical or mental threat to the woman.

The guidelines state that anyone who unlawfully performs an abortion is liable to criminal prosecution with a maximum penalty of life in prison. A person who is a 'secondary party' to such a termination faces the same penalty.

Medical assessment of women aged 18 or more seeking an abortion in the North would 'most appropriately' be carried out by a consultant general adult psychiatrist. A GP or consultant obstetrician 'who had prior knowledge of the woman and her clinical circumstances, and who is both experienced and competent in making mental health assessment in these situations, would also be appropriate to carry out the assessment'. For those under 18, a child and adolescent psychiatrist is deemed appropriate to make the assessment.

The guidelines say that while there is no legal right to refuse to take part in a lawful abortion, no one should compel staff who have a conscientious objection to abortion to take part in a termination. Where a doctor has a conscientious objection to abortion, he or she should make arrangements where the woman can be referred to another colleague.

DUP Junior Minister Jeffrey Donaldson said his party voted against the guidelines because it had reservations about some elements of the proposals. What was clear was that 'we will not be liberalising the law on abortion here'.

SDLP health spokeswoman Carmel Hanna welcomed the clarification of the clinical guidelines 'on the understanding that the absolute legal ban on abortion remains unchanged'.

'As a party that was born out of the civil rights movement, the SDLP believes that the right to life is the most basic right of all. That includes the right to life of the unborn,' she said.

UUP health spokesman John McAllister said the guidelines 'recognise and reaffirm the present legal situation – that, except where it is required to preserve the life of the woman, abortion is illegal in Northern Ireland'.

Bernadette Smyth, of Precious Life, said the proposals were an attempt 'by the back door' to legalise abortion in Northern Ireland. 'The guidelines fail to distinguish between direct abortion – when the child is intentionally killed – and indirect abortion – when the child dies unintentionally as a result of the mother receiving life-saving medical treatment,' she added.

Alliance for Choice group spokeswoman Goretti Horgan said, 'while the guidance does not change the law in any way, it does make it clear that women here have a right to end a pregnancy that threatens their physical or mental health'.

Her group would continue to campaign for the extension of the 1967 Abortion Act to Northern Ireland, she added.
21 March 2009

⇨ The above information is reprinted with kind permission from the *Irish Times*. Visit www.irishtimes.com for more information.

© *Irish Times 2009*

Public support for abortion in Northern Ireland

Information from the fpa

Nearly two-thirds of Northern Irish people polled (62 per cent) say that abortion should be legal in cases of rape or incest, according to a new survey from **fpa** in Northern Ireland. The strong support for women's right to choose is contrary to the myth that people in Northern Ireland do not want to see abortion available under any circumstances.

Ahead of a crucial vote on 22 October on an amendment to the Human Fertilisation and Embryology (HFE) Bill to extend the 1967 Abortion Act to Northern Ireland, the survey is an important revelation.

Only a minority of Northern Irish people (20 per cent) questioned in the survey said abortion should not be legal in cases of rape or incest. This shows how strong the support for choice in Northern Ireland is. A further 17 per cent said they did not know whether abortion should be legal in this circumstance or not.

Dr Audrey Simpson OBE, Director of **fpa** in Northern Ireland, said:

'It is time that the Northern Ireland Assembly faced up to the realities of the situation that people in Northern Ireland support the right to choose. These statistics cannot be ignored and show that MLAs have a responsibility to give women in Northern Ireland the choice to have an abortion.

'If the elected members of the Northern Ireland Assembly are not willing to listen to public opinion and give women in Northern Ireland the same human rights as women in the rest of the UK, then it is up to Westminster MPs to be the voice of Northern Irish women.'
20 October 2008

⇨ The above information is reprinted with kind permission from the **fpa**. Visit www.fpa.org.uk for more information.

© *fpa*

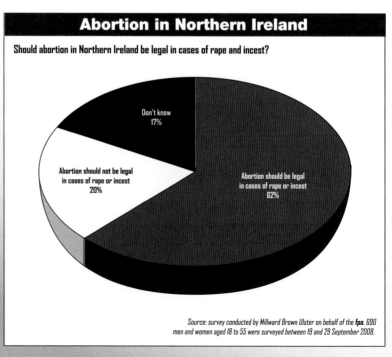

Abortion in Northern Ireland

Should abortion in Northern Ireland be legal in cases of rape and incest?

- Don't know 17%
- Abortion should not be legal in cases of rape or incest 20%
- Abortion should be legal in cases of rape or incest 62%

Source: survey conducted by Millward Brown Ulster on behalf of the fpa. 690 men and women aged 18 to 55 were surveyed between 19 and 29 September 2008.

Abortion and religion

Information from Education for Choice

Over a third of all pregnancies, across the world, are unplanned.[1] The discovery of an unplanned pregnancy affects all women differently. Each woman's circumstances are unique and there are sometimes reasons why she may not feel able to continue with a pregnancy.

Although some religions oppose abortion under all circumstances, many religions recognise the different factors that influence a woman's decision on how to proceed with a pregnancy and teach that there are some instances in which abortion is acceptable. Most religions agree that abortion is a last resort; they teach that the decision to have an abortion is a serious one and must not be taken lightly.

This article looks at some of the key moral questions that influence religious thought on abortion as well as looking at the teachings of some of the major world religions.

What are the key questions for people of different faiths?

When does life begin?
Not all religions define a particular moment when life begins but some, like Buddhism, Sikhism and Catholicism, teach that life begins at fertilisation – the moment that sperm meets egg. The Roman Catholic Church says that the fertilised egg is a sacred life, with as many rights as a baby, child or adult, and forbids abortion. Amongst Buddhists and Sikhs there is a variety of opinions on the morality of abortion.

Medical science tells us that a proportion of fertilised eggs do not become implanted in the woman's womb and that a large proportion of those that do (up to 25%) are lost naturally to miscarriage. This loss of 'life' is often not acknowledged in any formalised religious ritual – such

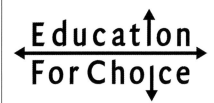

as a funeral – and in many cases the woman might not even know that she was pregnant or that she has miscarried.

Who has the greater right to life: the fetus or the woman?
The Roman Catholic Church says that abortion – 'the deliberate ending of a pregnancy' – is never acceptable, even to save the life of the woman. However, life-saving treatment can be carried out on a woman even if it will result in the death of the fetus. So, in this particular situation, the woman does have a greater right to life than the fetus.[2]

Over a third of all pregnancies, across the world, are unplanned

---

Most religions would choose to save the life of the woman even at the cost of the fetus. Even religions that are firmly opposed to abortion like the Greek and Russian Orthodox churches, Hinduism and Orthodox Judaism say that abortion is acceptable to save a woman's life.

Some religions go further than this and teach that the woman has the right to decide on the fate of the fetus even if continuing with the pregnancy does not directly threaten her life. It is argued by some Christians that God has given human beings free will and that we must respect the integrity of

the woman's conscience. To remove her choice is to deny that integrity and, in effect, her humanity.

Is abortion murder?
Most religions teach about the sanctity or sacredness of human life, but do not categorise abortion as murder.

Judaism, for example, only recognises the rights of a baby after the majority of the baby has left the woman's body, so although it teaches that abortion is morally wrong, it is not considered equivalent to murder.

Despite the general prohibition on killing – for example Judaism and Christianity teach 'Thou Shalt Not Kill' (Exodus and Deuteronomy), whilst Muslims believe '...whosoever kills a human being... it shall be as if he had killed all mankind.' (Quran 5:32) – most religions recognise that not all killing is murder. Killing in battle, in self-defence, as legal punishment or retribution is sanctioned by many religions.

Does the fetus have a soul?
Islam teaches that ensoulment (the moment that the soul enters the body of the fetus) takes place at 120 days and abortions after this time are considered to be more of a sin than early abortions.

The Roman Catholic Church used to teach that ensoulment takes place at 'quickening' when the woman starts to feel movement in her stomach (about 16 weeks). However, in 1869 the church changed its teaching and it now teaches that the soul is present from the moment of fertilisation.

Hindus believe that the fetus has a soul, although opinion is divided over what happens to the soul of an aborted fetus. Some believe that the soul, like all souls of the dead, will be reincarnated in another body.

Quakers believe that there is 'that of God in everyone' but do not give guidance on whether this applies to the fetus.

When does a fetus become a person?
This question is important because we do not give human rights (such as the right to life) to all living things (plants, animals etc) but only to people.

The earliest embryo contains the entire DNA code (genome) of the person that could develop from it, and some argue that its potential to become a person is enough to give it the rights of a fully developed person.

Others argue that a person is more than just the sum of its biological parts, and believe that a living person has characteristics that a fetus doesn't. These may include the ability to think and reason or the capacity to build relationships and to communicate.

Some believe that it is the ability of the fetus to exist independently of the woman that defines it as a person. They consider the fetus to have the right to life at the point where it is 'viable', meaning it can survive outside of the woman's womb. (British law recognises viability as an important indicator of personhood and gives greater rights to the fetus after this point in its development).

Most religions agree that gestation (the fetus growing in the womb) is a process of becoming a person and consequently teach that later abortions are morally worse than early abortions.

Where do world religions stand on abortion?
Some religions, notably the mono-theistic faiths, rely on one or two key texts and have clear doctrine on moral issues. Others, such as Hinduism and Buddhism, consist of collections of writings which are more open to interpretation. Some religions, like Islam, have maintained a relatively consistent teaching on abortion while others, like Roman Catholicism, have changed their ideas on abortion over time. The chart above aims to give a broad overview of the teaching of different religions on abortion.[3]

Religion, the law and practice

There is not always a connection between a country's main religion and its abortion laws.

⇨ Most Latin American countries prohibit or severely restrict abortion, which is in keeping with Roman Catholic teaching.

⇨ India, which has a majority Hindu population, has very liberal abortion laws that do not reflect mainstream Hindu teaching on abortion.

⇨ Egypt and Iran completely prohibit abortion despite the exception that Islam makes to preserve women's life or health.

The official teaching of a religion is not always reflected in the way its members actually live their lives. Many people feel that they must make decisions based on their own conscience and circumstances, even when they do not fit in with the official teachings of their religion or their own faith. Abortion is a good example of this as it takes place in every culture and every country in the world, often in opposition to the community's culture, religion or law. Statistics show that people of all religions have abortions and that the number of abortions that take place do not relate to the law or religion of the country.

Four million abortions a year take place in Latin America and 6,000 Irish women travel to Britain each year for abortions because it is prohibited in those countries by law and religion. 26% of the world's population live in countries where abortion is prohibited, but many of those countries have a high abortion rate. An estimated 70,000 women die each year through illegal abortions, demonstrating that prohibiting abortion does not prevent it from happening, but makes it unsafe by removing access to doctors and sanitary medical facilities.[4]

Teachings about abortion – an overview

Prohibited	The **Roman Catholic Church** teaches that abortion is always wrong. A Catholic who had an abortion could, in theory, be 'excommunicated' from the Church.	The **Jehovah's Witnesses** believe that abortion is always wrong.	The **Evangelical Christian** movement includes many who are totally opposed to abortion.
Very restricted	The **Russian and Greek Orthodox Churches** teach that abortion can only be justified to save a woman's life.	**Orthodox Judaism** believes that abortion can only be justified to save the woman's life or to protect her from the risk of serious and permanent injury.	**Hinduism** is opposed to abortion, but some Hindu texts approve of abortion to save a woman's life.
Limited	The **Church of England** considers that abortion is sometimes a 'necessary evil'. Later abortions are worse than early abortions.	**Islam** teaches that abortion is a sin which increases as pregnancy progresses, but allows for its use to save a woman's life or protect her health & in other limited circumstances.	**Liberal/Reform Judaism** leaves the decision to the woman and her partner, but is clear that abortion should not be used for 'trivial reasons'.
No written law	Some say that abortions break the first rule of **Buddhism**, which is to 'do no harm'. Others believe in compassion for the individual woman in this situation.	In **Sikhism**, decisions on contraception are left entirely up to the married couple and some also believe that abortion too is possible if both partners agree. Others say that it is forbidden.	There is no official teaching on abortion for **Quakers**. However, there is a great emphasis on personal conscience and the individual's capacity to make good decisions.
Individual decision	**Humanists** believe that the quality rather than the quantity of life is important and that there is nothing wrong in principle with abortion. Rational thought should direct our actions, so women have the choice to weigh up the pros and cons and make their own decisions.		The **Methodist Church** spoke out to highlight the dangers of illegal abortions before the law was changed in 1967. It teaches that you should have reverence for life and also have compassion for women who are not able to continue with a pregnancy.

Useful links

Catholicism
www.vatican.va
Hinduism Today
www.hinduismtoday.co.za
Anglican Church
www.cofe.anglican.org
Judaism
www.scjfaq.org
Islam
www.islam.org
Sikhism
www.sikhs.org.uk

Most of the political groups that oppose abortion do have a religious basis for their views, but there are also many religious people who support a woman's right to choose abortion and actively campaign to challenge negative attitudes towards abortion and women who have abortions. For more information on their arguments visit the websites below:

Catholics for Choice
www.cath4choice.org
Religious Coalition for Reproductive Choice
www.rcrc.org

These organisations provide general information on abortion:
Education for Choice
www.efc.org.uk
British Pregnancy Advisory Service
www.bpas.org
Marie Stopes
www.mariestopes.org.uk
Brook
www.brook.org.uk

For information on abortion worldwide:
The Alan Guttmacher Institute
www.agi-usa.org.

Centre for Reproductive Law and Policy
www.crlp.org.

Footnotes

1 According to the Safe Motherhood Initiative, 75 million of the 200 million pregnancies that take place around the world each year are unplanned. See www.safemotherhood.org for more information.
2 For example, a life-threatening ectopic pregnancy (in which the fertilised egg is implanted in the fallopian tube instead of the womb) can be ended by removing the whole fallopian tube, but not the fertilised egg on its own because according to Catholic law it must be the 'damaged' organ not the fetus that is being intentionally removed (*Abortion*, Catholic Truth Society: www.cts-online.org.uk).
3 For more detailed information and quotes from different religions, visit our website at www.efc.org.uk
4 World Health Organisation.

Glossary of terms

Doctrine
Strict teaching or rules.
Excommunicate
To exclude a person from membership or participation in the Church for breaking a religious code or law.
Fertilisation
When the sperm enters the egg.
Free will
The idea that human beings are free to choose their actions – good or bad – and are not forced to act by fate or pre-programmed to behave a certain way.
Gestation
The process of the development of the fetus which takes place throughout a woman's pregnancy, from implantation of the fertilised egg in the womb to birth.
Humanity
Distinguishes people from animals. It is normally used in a positive sense to mean human beings' ability to be thoughtful, rational and to care about the feelings of others.
Integrity
Honesty. Being true to your beliefs.
Monotheistic religions
Religions that teach there is a single God, such as Judaism, Christianity and Islam. Religions that believe in more than one God (like Hinduism) are polytheistic.
Personhood
Being more than just a body, but having thoughts and feelings.

Prohibited
Not allowed – banned.
Quickening
An old-fashioned word for the time when the woman can feel the fetus begin to move within her womb. This normally takes place at around 16 weeks.
Reincarnation
The belief that when a person dies, their soul or spirit is born again in another body or another form.
Retribution
A severe punishment or revenge. An example of this would be the Old Testament's 'an eye for an eye' in which the punishment directly reflects the crime.
Sanctity
The sanctity of human life refers to the idea that human life is sacred or holy – that it is owed special protection and respect.
Viability
The point at which a fetus might be able, with medical support, to exist outside of the woman's womb.

⇨ The above information is reprinted with kind permission from Education for Choice. Visit www.efc.org.uk for more information.
© *Education for Choice*

A humanist discussion of abortion

Information from the British Humanist Association

Humanists seek to live good lives without religious or superstitious beliefs. They use reason, experience and respect for others when thinking about moral issues, not obedience to dogmatic rules. So in thinking about abortion a humanist would consider the evidence, the probable consequences, and the rights and wishes of everyone involved, trying to find the kindest course of action or the one that would do the least harm.

Abortion is an issue that demonstrates the difficulties of rigid rules in moral decision making. Medical science has advanced to the point where we have options that were unthinkable even a few generations ago and where old rules cannot cope with new facts.

Some medical facts

⇨ Some very premature babies can now be kept alive, which has altered ideas about when foetuses become human beings with human rights. The law in England and Wales is based on the fact that after 24 weeks the foetus is often viable, in that with medical assistance it can survive outside the womb.
⇨ Many illnesses and disabilities can now be diagnosed long before birth.
⇨ Some very ill or disabled babies who would probably once have died before or shortly after birth can now be kept alive.
⇨ The sex of a foetus can be known well before birth (and some parents would like to be able to choose the sex of their child).
⇨ Genetic research makes it increasingly likely that parents will be able to know, or even to choose, other characteristics for their

unborn child. A few will want to reject some foetuses.

⇨ Abortions can be performed safely, though they can occasionally cause medical or psychological problems.

These are in themselves morally neutral medical facts, but they bring with them the necessity to make moral choices and to consider who should make those choices. Doctors? Politicians? Religious leaders? Medical ethics committees? Individual women? Their partners?

Some views on abortion

Some examples of contemporary rules and views about abortion will perhaps demonstrate the complexity of the problem.

Some religious people think that all human life is sacred, that life begins at conception, and so abortion is always wrong (and some also believe that contraception is wrong, which leads to even more unwanted pregnancies). But a humanist would argue that the idea of 'sacredness' is unhelpful if one has to choose between risking the life of the mother or the life of the unborn foetus. (This is very rare these days, and the choice is most often about the quality of life of either the mother or the foetus or both.)

People often argue that it is not for doctors to 'play God' and that it is for God to decide matters of life and death. But it could be said that all medical interventions are 'playing God' (even your childhood vaccinations may have kept you alive longer than 'God' planned) so we have to decide for ourselves how we use medical powers. Arguments which

Questions to think about and discuss

⇨ Is abortion in the case of conception after rape more justified than other abortions?

⇨ Would a humanist favour abortion if a woman wanted one because her pregnancy was interfering with her holiday plans? Why (not)?

⇨ Why do humanists think contraception is better than abortion?

⇨ Are there any good arguments against adoption of unwanted babies?

⇨ Should doctors and nurses impose their moral views on patients? Yes? Sometimes? Never?

⇨ Should religious people impose their views on abortion on non-religious people? Yes? Sometimes? Never?

⇨ Should parents be able to choose the sex of their child? Should they be able to abort a foetus of the 'wrong' sex?

⇨ At what point does a foetus become a human being? Does this affect the humanist view of abortion? Does this affect your view of abortion?

⇨ Can infanticide ever be right?

⇨ Should abortion ever be carried out on a non-consenting woman, e.g. one too young to give legal consent or one in a coma?

⇨ How are you deciding your answers to these questions? What principles and arguments influence your answers?

⇨ How is the humanist view on this issue similar to that of other worldviews you have come across? How is it different?

invoke God are unconvincing to those who do not believe in gods, and laws should not be based on claims which rely on religious faith.

Some (non-religious) moral philosophers have argued that full consciousness begins only after birth or even later, and so foetuses and infants are not full human beings with human rights.

Doctors have a range of opinions on abortion, but tend to give the medical interests of the mother (which may include her mental health) the most weight when making decisions.

Some doctors and nurses dislike carrying out abortions because they

feel that their job is to save life, not to destroy it.

Some people believe that a woman has absolute rights over her own body which override those of any unborn foetus. You might like to read Judith Jarvis Thomson's 'A Defense of Abortion' (see bibliography over page) which states a feminist case for abortion very clearly.

The law in England, Scotland and Wales permits abortion before the 24th week of pregnancy if two doctors agree that there is a risk to the life or the mental or physical health of the mother if the pregnancy continues, or there will be a risk to the mental or physical health of other children in the family. However, there is no time limit if there is a substantial risk that the baby will be born severely disabled, or there is a grave risk of death or permanent injury (mental or physical) to the mother. In effect this means that almost every woman who wants an abortion and is persistent in seeking one before the 24th week can obtain one. However, some women who do not realise that they are pregnant until too late (perhaps because they are very young or because they are menopausal) may not be able to have abortions though they would have qualified on other grounds.

The humanist view

The current law is permissive: it does not impose abortion on anyone who does not want one or does not want to perform one. So even within the law, individuals have to make moral choices. How do humanists pick their way between these conflicting ideas? There is not one, correct humanist view on abortion. However, humanists tend to converge on a liberal, 'pro-choice' stance. Humanists value happiness and personal choice, and many actively campaigned for legalised abortion in the 1960s. Although humanists do not think all life is 'sacred' they do respect life, and much in this debate hinges on when one thinks human life begins. Humanists tend to think that – on the basis of scientific evidence about foetal development – a foetus does not become a person, with its own feelings and rights, until well after conception.

Because humanists take happiness and suffering as foremost moral considerations, quality of life will often trump the preservation of life at all costs, if the two come into conflict. (Assisted dying is another example.) The probable quality of life of the baby, the woman, rights and wishes of the father and the rest of the family, and the doctors and nurses involved, would all have to be given due weight. There is plenty of room for debate about how much weight each individual should have, but most humanists put the interests of the woman first, since she would have to complete the pregnancy and probably care for the baby, whose happiness would largely depend on hers. She also exists already with other responsibilities and rights and feelings that can be taken into account – unlike those of the unborn foetus which cannot be so surely ascertained.

Of course, all possible options should be explored and decisions should be informed ones. Adoption of the unwanted baby might be the best solution in some cases, or on reflection a woman might decide that she could look after a sick or disabled child. Or she might decide that she cannot offer this child a life worth living and abortion is the better choice. She will need to consider the long-term effects as well as the immediate ones. It is unlikely to be an easy decision, and requiring an abortion is a situation that most women would prefer to avoid.

For society as a whole, as well as for the children themselves, it is better if every child is a wanted child. However, abortion is not the best way of avoiding unwanted children, and improved sex education, easily available contraception, and better education and opportunities for young women, can all help to reduce the number of abortions. But as long as abortion is needed as a last resort, most humanists would agree that society should provide safe, legal facilities. The alternatives, which would inevitably include illegal abortions, are far worse.

Further reading

⇨ Mary Warnock, *An Intelligent Person's Guide to Ethics* (Duckworth)

⇨ Jonathan Glover, *Causing Death and Saving Lives* (Penguin)

⇨ Peter Singer, *Practical Ethics* (Cambridge University Press)

⇨ Judith Jarvis Thomson, (1971), 'A Defense of Abortion', widely reprinted e.g. in Michael Palmer, *Moral Problems* (Lutterworth)

⇨ The above information is reprinted with kind permission from the British Humanist Association. Visit www.humanism.org.uk for more information.

© British Humanist Association

Hard questions

Information from Life

Abortion and rape

Rape is a truly horrific crime against women. Whether or not pregnancy has resulted, the woman needs a lot of help and support to recover from the experience. It can seem as though a child conceived as a result will be a constant reminder of the attack and for this reason abortion is often seen as the obvious response to a sexual assault pregnancy. Statistics suggest that pregnancy occurs in around 5% of rape cases, the subsequent abortion rate represents a tiny fraction of the 200,000 abortions carried out in the UK each year.

⇨ At the heart of the pro-life case is a simple conviction: that an unborn child, at whatever stage

Life
LOVING LIFE, OFFERING HOPE

of development, is a human being with as much right to life as you or I. The circumstances in which the unborn child came into the world do not alter our recognition of the child's humanity. Surely all of us deserve the chance to be born and make something of our life, however we were conceived?

⇨ Why should the child suffer the death penalty when he/she is entirely innocent? We cannot discriminate against an unborn child simply because of the actions of their father. Many children have to live with parents who are inadequate, cruel or violent. Life is not easy for these children, but we do not say that their lives are worthless because of their parents' failings and problems.

⇨ We may think that abortion is the best way for a woman to begin to move on from the trauma of rape; however, abortion cannot undo the fact that the rape happened. The abortion can bring with it a new set of problems. Some women report that the trauma and emotional intensity of abortion exacerbate their existing difficulties.

⇨ We recognise at LIFE that a pregnancy resulting from rape is a traumatic and devastating situation. But a woman facing a crisis pregnancy as a result of rape need not face the situation alone. LIFE provides a whole range of services, including practical and emotional support and confidential counselling.

⇨ In society we are quick to judge the situation and view the child merely as a rapist's offspring, forgetting that the child is also the mother's son or daughter. A huge amount of pressure can be put on the woman to have an abortion and move on.

One girl, who wished to remain anonymous, told us her story:

'...I can honestly say that keeping my daughter was a great decision, and I really enjoy being a mother. Although she was conceived in traumatic circumstances, I came to understand that she had done nothing wrong and was not responsible for the way she came into the world.

'Some people have judged me harshly for carrying the child of a rapist; but when I look at my daughter I don't see the face of my rapist – I see my beautiful daughter, who I love. She is the proof that something good can come from something terrible...'

Abortion and disability

Tests for disability

1 Chorionic villus sampling (CVS): this tests a tiny part of the placenta in the early stages of pregnancy.

2 Alphafetoprotein test (AFP): widely used, tests a mothers blood sample at about 16 weeks.

3 Amniocentesis test: involves removing some of the amniotic fluid from around the child, by syringe at about 18 weeks (has at least a 1% risk of causing miscarriage).

4 Ultrasound scanning: involves 'bouncing' sound waves off the baby to produce a moving picture on a monitor screen, revealing the development of the child.

Pre-natal screening is not wholly reliable; it is reckoned that 10% of diagnoses are incorrect.

Even if the child is found to be at risk of disability, it can be hard to predict the degree of disability.

⇨ However and whenever disability is detected the child needs help with his/her difficulties and the family needs support and sometimes practical help.

⇨ A person with a disability has the same right to life as any other member of society. Aborting children because they have or might have a disability is the ultimate form of discrimination.

⇨ In the UK it is legally permitted to abort a baby up to birth on grounds of disability. Acceptance of abortion on these grounds has led to the killing of unborn disabled children who are unwanted or rejected. If pre-natal screening reveals a disability, parents are often put under pressure to opt for an abortion.

⇨ Many people argue in favour of aborting disabled babies on the grounds that they will have 'a poor quality of life'. How can anyone know this? How can anyone have the right to pre-judge the quality of someone else's life before they are even born?

⇨ It is one of today's biggest contradictions that just as we have really begun to look after disabled people as never before, providing privileged parking spaces, protected jobs, specially adapted work environments etc, we are devising increasingly more ruthless methods of searching out and destroying unborn disabled people.

The Disability Rights Commission (DRC) are extremely concerned about this law as it reinforces discrimination against people with disability. In 2001, the DRC stated that:

'The section is offensive to many people. It reinforces negative stereotypes of disability and there is substantial support for the view that to permit terminations at any point during a pregnancy on the grounds of risk of disability, while time limits apply to other grounds set out in the abortion act, is incompatible with valuing disability and non-disability equally.'

Abortion to save the mother's life

In years gone by, the choice between saving the life of the mother or the child was not uncommon. Medicine and science have advanced so far that this need not be the case these days.

⇨ There are nowadays very few occasions where the life of the mother is threatened by pregnancy. Even in this rare situation, the child can be delivered and given the chance to survive.

⇨ Children delivered a little over halfway through the pregnancy now have a much better chance of survival because of the skill of doctors and the facilities available in special-care baby units.

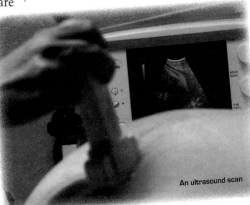
An ultrasound scan

⇨ Medical intervention to save the life of the mother that results in the death of the child as an expected but not intended side effect is not a direct abortion, e.g. in the case of ectopic pregnancy. In this situation the baby begins to develop in the mother's fallopian tube and has to be removed or the fallopian tube will rupture and cause the death of the mother. In this case the baby dies as the result of a condition where nothing else can be done, but a direct choice is not taken to end the life of one in favour of another.

Backstreet abortion

This term is usually used to describe illegal abortions. Backstreet abortions played a major role in the legalisation of abortion in the first place. Pro-abortion campaigners claimed that legalising abortion was necessary to stop thousands of dangerous abortions taking place which caused injury and death for many desperate women.

This argument, accompanied by alarming statistics, was instrumental in convincing politicians to change the law on abortion, but there is little evidence to suggest that backstreet abortion was the problem some campaigners claimed it to be. In fact, the number of women in danger after backstreet abortion was in decline in the years leading up to the 1967 abortion act. Dr Bernard Nathanson, co-founder of the United States pro-abortion group NARAL (National Association for the Repeal of Abortion Laws), admitted that the drive to legalise abortion was based on the invention of false statistics. He said:

'We aroused enough sympathy to sell our program of permissive abortion by fabricating the number of illegal abortions done annually in the US. The actual figure was approaching 100,000 but the figure we gave to the media repeatedly was 1,000,000.

Repeating the big lie often enough convinces the public. The number of women dying from illegal abortions was around 200-250 annually. The figure we constantly fed to the media was 10,000.'
Bernard Nathanson, Confessions of an Ex-Abortionist

A law banning abortion would not stop all women from having abortions. But it would be a powerful statement about the value of human life and about the ideals of our society. Rape is illegal. Why? Not because we think that by making rape illegal we will completely stop rape from happening, but because we recognise that rape is wrong and bad for society and we want to discourage people from committing rape by any means possible. The same can be said for theft, assault, drink-driving and so on.

The law matters because it is a statement of the kind of society we want to build, and the society that LIFE wants to build is one that respects and protects the dignity of each and every human being,

especially the small, the vulnerable and those who suffer exploitation and discrimination. Legal abortion radically undermines the principle of equality before the law.

There are those who say that this position is uncaring. We disagree. LIFE is at the forefront of caring for women in crisis pregnancy. We recognise that both a woman and her unborn child need our support, love and care.

It is true that many women suffer after illegal abortions. But remember, too, that in every single abortion, whether legal or illegal, a human life is taken. And women often suffer after legal abortions. You can find out more about the consequences of abortion for some women in other LIFE literature.

⇨ The above information is re-printed with kind permission from Life. Visit www.lifecharity.org.uk for more information on this and other related topics.

© Life

'It is very difficult to keep a 24-week baby alive'

The fact that it has become possible to keep alive the occasional premature child born as early as 24 weeks into their gestation has played a key role in the recent debate over abortion, a point acknowledged by Dr Hussein Mehmet, honorary reader in neuroscience at Imperial College London. 'It did make me think very carefully about this issue,' he told *The Observer*.

In 1967, when the Abortion Act was passed, it was assumed that the age of viability for a foetus was 28 weeks, a limit previously enshrined in the 1929 Infant Life Preservation Act. However, over the next two decades the development of drugs that help premature babies to breathe in incubators, and the setting up of neo-natal clinics to care for these early-born babies across the country, brought the age of viability down to 24 weeks.

By Robin McKie

As a result, it was decided to change the abortion limit from 28 to 24 weeks when parliament debated the 1990 Human Fertilisation and Embryology Act. Since then, anti-abortion campaigners have argued that further improvements in viability would help them to press for further changes in the time limit.

'At present the age around 24 weeks remains a viability and I can see no reason to change the time limit'

However, this has proved to be a forlorn hope, as Mehmet makes clear.

'It is very, very difficult to keep a 24-week baby alive,' he says. 'If you look at magnetic resonance image scans of babies at 24 weeks, you can see their brains are still not properly developed. More to the point, they do not catch up if we do manage to keep them alive. A lot of these children tend to have a very poor quality of life.'

For this reason, Mehmet – while initially hesitant – can see no reason to change the legal limit for abortions. 'At present the age around 24 weeks remains a viability and I can see no reason to change the time limit. Indeed, if it is brought down, the only people who would suffer would be women who discover late in pregnancy that they are carrying a foetus that has serious abnormalities but who could no longer get an abortion.'
⇨ This article first appeared in *The Observer*, 18 May 2008.
© Guardian Newspapers Limited 2009

Many born within abortion limit survive

Many children are surviving after being born within the legal limit for abortion, official figures have disclosed

By James Kirkup

Department of Health data show that 435 children were born after less than 24 weeks of pregnancy during 2005. Of those, 52 survived for at least a year.

The figures will be used by pro-life campaigners as further proof of the need to cut the abortion time limit when MPs vote on the issue in the coming weeks.

The current time limit of 24 weeks was laid down by Parliament in 1990. As early as next month, MPs will vote on a range of amendments to cut the limit.

The Human Fertilisation and Embryology Bill will give MPs their first full opportunity to vote on abortion laws since 1990.

All parties have given their members a free vote on the issue, and MPs are expecting a close vote on moves to cut the time limit to 20 weeks.

Gordon Brown, the Prime Minister, has signalled that he will oppose any cut in the time limit.

David Cameron, the Tory leader, has said that he is prepared to vote for a 20-week limit.

The DoH figures for babies' survival were released to David Amess, a pro-life Conservative MP, in a written parliamentary answer.

The data, for births in England and Wales, showed that eight of the 152 children born after 22 weeks' gestation lived for a year or more.

At 23 weeks, 44 of 283 children survived. At 24 weeks, almost half – 198 of 474 – of babies survived. Of the 201,173 abortions in England and Wales in 2006, 1,262 were at 22 weeks or more.

Scientists are divided about campaigners' claims that survival rates for babies born before 24 weeks have increased.

Epicure 2, a Government-funded study into the survival rates of premature babies based on 1995 figures, has suggested that the chance of survival was between 10 and 15 per cent, and the British Association of Perinatal Medicine has suggested that survival rates have not changed significantly since then.

John Wyatt, a University College London professor and a member of the anti-abortion Christian Medical Fellowship, has claimed that survival rates are as high as 42 per cent at 23 weeks and 72 per cent at 24 weeks' gestation.

Anti-abortion campaigners point out that survival rates can be even higher in specialist hospital units.

Last month a separate study, carried out at University College London Hospital, found that one-third of babies born between 22 and 25 weeks' gestation survived in the early 1980s but this had risen to 71 per cent by the late 1990s.

Julia Millington of the ProLife Alliance, which campaigns for tighter abortion laws, said the survival figures underlined the case for change.

'There have been vast improvements in neo-natal care since the upper time limit for abortion was last set by Parliament, and we are now routinely aborting babies that would have a good chance of survival in specialist hospitals,' she said.

Mr Brown was yesterday challenged by Ian Paisley, the former First Minister of Northern Ireland, not to allow the Embryology Bill to liberalise abortion laws 'by the backdoor'.

The Prime Minister replied: 'I do not believe the House will want to change its mind on this issue, but it is a matter for the whole House.'

Nadine Dorries, a Tory backbencher who is campaigning for lower abortion time limits, said the national figures masked a 'postcode lottery' where properly equipped neonatal units could deliver much higher survival rates for premature babies.

She added: 'Even more viable babies are being aborted than these figures would suggest. If you go into labour at 22 weeks, there is something wrong with you or your baby. Most babies aborted at 22 weeks are healthy, so their survival chances would be even higher.'

Some late-term abortions are carried out because foetuses are showing signs of defects, including club feet and cleft palates.

In 2004, it emerged that a baby was aborted at 28 weeks after scans showed it had a cleft palate.

18 April 2008

© *Telegraph Group Limited, London 2008*

Third of GPs 'would not offer abortion'

GP survey calls whole Department of Health abortion strategy into question, says CMF

The Christian Medical Fellowship says that today's nationwide survey of GPs confirms that allowing early abortions in GP surgeries would radically change family medicine and will not be in the best interests of women with crisis pregnancies.

The *GP Newspaper*'s survey of 480 UK GPs found a third would refuse to work in a surgery or polyclinic offering abortion, more than half believed offering such abortions would increase the total rate and 61% did not believe practices should be offering such services at all.

The survey also revealed that most GPs do not favour further liberalisation of the abortion law. Nearly half want the current 24-week limit lowered, with one in ten calling for it to be cut to 15 weeks or less, and 75% did not want the numbers of doctors' signatures required for abortion reduced from two to one.

Dr Trevor Stammers, CMF Chairman and a GP in south London, had previously said to *GP Newspaper* that he would 'certainly be forced to resign from practice if the PCT [Primary Care Trust] compels any building in which I practise to carry out abortions. I will not be alone in doing this.'

He added today: 'This extensive survey confirms my position and shows that many GPs are so seriously concerned about extending abortion to GP premises that the whole Department of Health strategy is called into question. Many GPs object to being involved in abortion and family medical practice is simply not the right context for it. Rather than this proposed extension of abortion into every local community, CMF supports both access to counselling that is independent of abortion provision and increasing support services for women who wish to continue with an unplanned pregnancy. One in three women will change their minds about abortion if given time, space and support to make a fully informed decision about an unplanned pregnancy.'

The *GP Newspaper*'s survey of 480 UK GPs found a third would refuse to work in a surgery or polyclinic offering abortion

---

CMF General Secretary Dr Peter Saunders said, 'If GP surgeries are to be used for carrying out abortions, what is that saying about family medicine? What confusion will this create in patients' minds when their "family doctor" is treating illness in one consulting room and ending life in another? This is abortion liberalisation by stealth and most GPs believe it will increase the number of abortions, including many where the women concerned might have chosen otherwise. The government must listen to the voices of frontline doctors, most of whom do not believe GP surgeries should be offering abortion at all and many of whom would refuse to work in such surgeries. This move is both unwanted and unnecessary and should not be foisted upon GPs.'

CMF is also a member of the Alive and Kicking Alliance, representing 12 organisations and over two million people, which is supporting amendments to the Abortion Act that will help to reduce substantially the number of abortions in the UK. *10 February 2009*

⇨ The above information is reprinted with kind permission from the Christian Medical Fellowship. Visit www.cmf.org.uk for more information.

© *Christian Medical Fellowship*

Should abortion be legal?

To what extent do you agree or disagree with the following statement? 'It should be legal for a woman to have an abortion when she has an unwanted pregnancy.'

- Strongly disagree 7%
- Don't know 4%
- Prefer not to say 3%
- Disagree 7%
- Neither agree nor disagree 16%
- Strongly agree 32%
- Agree 31%

Sample size: 1983. Fieldwork: 14-16 November 2007. Source: YouGov (www.yougov.com)

GP abortion poll 'not representative'

Online poll conducted by *GP magazine* 'not representative', claims Department of Health

A small online poll conducted by *GP magazine* claims that one in three family doctors in England and Wales would refuse to work in surgeries or clinics that offered abortions.

And almost two in three, 61 per cent, who responded to the survey do not believe that practices should be offering them at all, the *Daily Telegraph* reports.

Medical terminations up to nine weeks could be offered in surgeries across the country after pilot studies showed that they were safe. In January, some local healthcare trusts said that they were considering plans to offer the service, in which doctors and nurses from BPAS provide pregnancy consultations and early medical abortion from GPs' premises.

This new poll suggests that some GPs oppose this move. The poll, of 480 family doctors, also shows that more than half of them believe that offering the terminations outside hospitals will increase the overall abortion rate. Almost half of those who took part in the survey also wanted to see the current 24-week limit for abortion lowered, and one in ten called for it to be set at 15 weeks or less. The survey also shows that three in four respondents believe that the number of doctors' signatures required for an abortion should remain at two and not be cut to just one, as has been suggested.

Dr Sarah Jarvis, from the Royal College of GPs, has reportedly warned that abortions would be 'trivialised' by becoming available in doctors' surgeries.

Dr Trevor Stammers, chairman of the Christian Medical Fellowship and a GP in south London, said:

'Medical abortions are not a harmless procedure. I will play no part in brutalising women in such a way and will do all I can to try and help women to see that abortion may not be the best way out in the long run.'

However, a spokesman for the Department of Health said:

'This is an extremely small survey of 480 GPs out of the 40,000 plus GPs working in the UK and therefore may not be fully representative. A much larger survey by Marie Stopes International of more than 7,000 GPs has shown that 82 per cent describe themselves as "pro-choice".

'Providing early medical abortion in a community setting is about increasing the choice of method and location as well as improving early access to abortions. Evidence shows that earlier abortions carry less risk of complications – it is not about increasing the number of abortions.'

Ann Furedi, chief executive of BPAS, described the survey results as 'disappointingly negative' and said there was no evidence that offering EMA pushed up the total number of abortions:

'I don't think this survey is reflective of what GPs across the country think. It's a small sample that requires GPs to go online to answer the survey and we know that organisations that are against abortion are very good at mobilising their members to respond.'

Ms Furedi said there were three reasons why some GPs may object to providing EMA in primary care, including that they were unfamiliar with the new technology in EMA, that there would be a need for ongoing care of the woman such as counselling, and that GPs were worried about how it would fit with their current workload. She added:

'There is no doubt about it that, in circumstances where abortions are legal, the earlier it can be provided the better. There is no evidence to show that when EMA is available it increases the number of abortions. We provide over 15,000 EMA procedures a year but that does not mean we are doing absolutely more abortions. It means that we are doing fewer abortions at 10, 11 and 12 weeks.'

11 February 2009

⇨ The above information is reprinted with kind permission from *Abortion Review*, a professional journal produced by the British Pregnancy Advisory Service (BPAS). Visit www.bpas.org for more information.

© *British Pregnancy Advisory Service (BPAS)*

Conscientious objection

Charles Williams considers whether doctors have a right to stand by their moral convictions on abortion

In October 2007 a small number of UK Muslim medical students made the headlines for missing lectures about sexually transmitted diseases and alcohol on moral grounds.[1] In November a general practitioner, Tammie Downes, was investigated by the General Medical Council after disclosing in a newspaper interview her success in dissuading several women from having abortions.[2]

These stories highlight a conflict between morality and medicine. What are we to make of doctors whose morals compel them to opt out of certain tasks? Judgmental moralisers? Workshy cowards? Or courageous individuals who risk career progression for higher ideals?

Debating abortion

One flash point in the morals-medicine minefield is abortion. Before 1967 abortion was illegal in the United Kingdom but was widely practised, unsafely, in unhygienic backstreet 'clinics.' The Abortion Act 1967 decriminalised abortion in certain circumstances. The act also includes a clause that states that 'no person shall be under any duty, whether by contract or by any statutory or other legal requirement, to participate in any treatment authorised by this act to which he has a conscientious objection'. Very few people actively call for this clause to be repealed, but some think that doctors who have a problem with taking part in abortion should reassess their commitment to medicine or at least stay away from specialities such as obstetrics and gynaecology.

More and more abortions are taking place,[2] but fewer doctors are willing to perform them. The Royal College of Obstetricians and Gynaecologists is worried at the fall in the number of young doctors willing to perform abortions,[3] and the British Pregnancy Advisory Service, which carries out a quarter of terminations in England, has said that in five years' time women's access to abortion may be 'severely restricted.'[3] This coincides with a more widespread recruitment crisis: according to the Royal College the number of trainees entering the speciality needs to treble.[4] One opinion is that doctors who opt out because of conscientious objection are putting their colleagues in an unfair position.

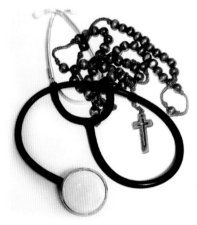

Should doctors be allowed to refuse to perform abortions for moral or religious reasons?

I have been urged to 'think about the poor gynaecologist being forced to do all the abortions because her colleagues refuse'. Some people believe that doctors in obstetrics and gynaecology should forgo their right to conscientious objection. Is abortion a duty of the gynaecologist so that you should opt for a different speciality if you have a conscientious objection to abortion?

In fact, the job of the obstetrician and gynaecologist is varied, and there are many opportunities for subspecialisation. It does not seem at all self-evident that a conscientious objection to abortion should rule out a career in the speciality.

Legality and justness

Abortion is legal, and doctors exist to serve patients. So should a doctor be required to provide a service if women are legally entitled to it? The ethicist Julian Savulescu equates the legality of an act with its justness in a passionate article against conscientious objection.[5] History, however, tells us that such an argument does not stand. Doctors in Nazi Germany took part in the sterilisation of patients with epilepsy and schizophrenia and in the murder of old, disabled and other burdensome patients, doing their duty under laws that sanctioned active euthanasia. Any praise we give to medics in that regime rightly belongs to the conscientious objectors.

Many of our present day counterparts around the world are placed in situations with which we might be profoundly uncomfortable. These include the death penalty and torture. If the law says that death is the appropriate penalty for certain crimes, should a state-registered doctor be able to opt out of his duty to give the lethal injection? If torture is considered a reasonable way to extract information from a criminal, as it seems to be in Guantanamo Bay, should the medic treat a prisoner, patching him up enough for further interrogation? Most of us hope for the courage to conscientiously object in these situations.

Statutory law and moral law are not synonymous in content because statutory law can change with time. The Declaration of Geneva used to affirm the 'utmost respect of human life from the time of its conception'. Since 1984 'from the time of its conception' has been absent. In 1983 the doctor who is against abortion is in agreement with the codified morals of his profession, but in 1984 it is a grey area. Morality is surely not so fickle?

When it comes to abortion, following the law is no simple thing either. The wording of the UK abortion law is ambiguous. It does not provide details about the circumstances in which abortion is permitted or not, but it requires doctors to weigh up the risks.

But how do we compare the risk to a woman's mental health of continuing a pregnancy with terminating it? Some research shows that abortion has harmful psychological sequelae,[6,7] although the Royal College of Psychiatrists believes the evidence base is inconclusive.[8] How great a risk is 'substantial'? How bad must a physical or mental abnormality be to constitute a serious handicap? Even a doctor willing to be involved in legal abortions may have to face questions of conscience.

Patients' rights and doctors' rights

Patient autonomy is paramount, but physician autonomy is also enshrined in law. The United Nations Universal Declaration of Human Rights declares the universal right to freedom of conscience. The Human Rights Act affirms the right to 'freedom of thought, conscience, and religion'. The BMA also acknowledges this right, accepting that it must be held in balance with patients' rights.[9]

Evan Harris, a doctor and Liberal Democrat Member of Parliament, believes that doctors conscientiously opposed to abortion cannot provide balanced counsel to patients seeking an abortion and should therefore 'refer them to another doctor immediately for that consultation'. He criticised Tammie Downes, introduced at the beginning of this article, for trying to persuade patients to go in one direction only and boasting of her 'success' in a national newspaper.

Downes responded, 'I don't try to persuade anybody. I give them the facts and allow them space to think through the decision that they are making.' She says that whether or not to have an abortion 'has to be the mother's choice. I have no right to make that choice for them.' But she believes that it is her 'duty as a doctor to help a woman make that choice.'[10]

What makes a valid claim?

There will always be disagreement about what constitutes reasonable grounds to opt out of providing a service. People's different world views lead them to profoundly different takes on morality. It is not immediately obvious what constitutes

a legitimate claim for conscientious objection in practice.

All doctors agree to sacrifice some of their personal autonomy when embarking on a career in medicine because the duties of the doctor state that we must make care of our patient our first concern, and we must treat our patients with respect, whatever our life choices and beliefs. A legitimate claim for conscientious objection should be based on a deeply held objection to what the patient is asking the doctor to do, not what the patient has done or how the patient lives.

Conclusion

The GMC acknowledges the central role of personal, cultural, and religious values and beliefs in the lives of doctors and patients in its latest guidance on this issue.[11] It reiterates the core message of Good Medical Practice,[12] that doctors must show respect for human life and that doctors must not discriminate against patients. Doctors should inform patients of any potential conscientious objection to a treatment and ensure that patients have sufficient information about how to see another doctor if they wish to do so. So the GMC affirms the right to conscientious objection.

Conscientious objection in medicine is rarely an easy way out. It may add to paperwork, complicate relationships with colleagues, and leave the doctor feeling vulnerable and isolated. However, history shows that rapid changes of law is reason enough to uphold the doctor's right to raise conscientious objection. We may never all agree on what is the right thing to do in difficult clinical and moral situations. But we need more doctors, not fewer, who are willing to defend what they think is right.

By Charles Williams, fifth year medical student ,Trinity College, Oxford University.

References

1 Foggo and Tahir. 'Muslim students get picky.' *Sunday Times* October 7, 2007
2 Department of Health Abortion Statistics, England and Wales: 2006. [Online]. Available from: http://www.dh.gov.uk/en/Publicationsandstatistics/Publications/PublicationsStatistics/DH_075697 [Accessed: 12 February 2008]
3 The *Mail on Sunday*. 'GP who made eight women think again.' [Online]. Available from: http://www.mailonsunday.co.uk/pages/live/articles/news/news.html?in_article_id=452319&in_page_id=1770the [Accessed: 12 February 2008]
4 Laurance, J. 'Abortion crisis as doctors refuse to perform surgery.' *The Independent* 16 April 2007
5 BMJ. 'UK trainee doctors spurn obstetrics and gynaecology.' [Online]. Available from: http://www.bmj.com/cgi/content/full/332/7537/323-c/DC1 [Accessed: 12 February 2008]
6 Savulescu, J. 'Conscientious objection in medicine.' BMJ 2006;332:294-297
7 BMA. 'Impact of Human Rights Act 1998 on medical decision making.' [Online]. Available from: http://www.bma.org.uk/ap.nsf/Content/HumanRightsAct~relevant~article9 [Accessed: 12 February 2008]
8 Reardon et al. 'Psychiatric admissions of low-income women following abortion and childbirth.' CMAJ. 2003; 168(10):1253-6
9 Fergusson DM, Horwood LJ, Ridder EM. 'Abortion in young women and subsequent mental health.' *J Child Psychol Psychiatry* 2006; 47:16-24
10 GMC. 'Personal Belief and Medical Practice' (2008) [Online]. Available from: http://www.gmc-uk.org/guidance/ethical_guidance/personal_beliefs/personal_beliefs.asp [Accessed: 1 April 2008]
11 GMC. 'Good Medical Practice' (2006) [Online]. Available from: http://www.gmc-uk.org/guidance/good_medical_practice/duties_of_a_doctor.asp [Accessed: 20 March 2008]

July 2008

⇨ The above information is reprinted with kind permission from Student BMJ. Visit http://student.bmj.com for more information.

© *Student BMJ*

Women want a stricter abortion law

Information from the Christian Institute

As MPs prepare to vote on abortion, a new opinion poll indicates that women strongly back a reduction in the abortion time limit.

⇨ Three in four women (73 per cent) think the abortion limit should be reduced to 20 weeks or lower to be more in line with EU countries.

⇨ 72 per cent of women (and more than half of the general public) also want a lower abortion time limit in light of the survival rates of babies born before 24 weeks.

⇨ 92 per cent of women (and 89 per cent of the general public) agree that women should have a statutory legal right to be told of all the physical and psychological risks known to be associated with abortion.

The figures are the result of a poll conducted on behalf of the Christian Institute by polling company ComRes.

The viability of premature babies

In the last year for which figures are available, Government statistics show that 52 babies survived having been born earlier than 24 weeks. At one specialist neo-natal unit in Britain, five out of seven babies born at 22 weeks gestation survived. In light of this:

⇨ 72 per cent of women (60 per cent of people) said the time limit should be decreased.

⇨ 70 per cent of 25- to 34-year-olds said the time limit should be decreased.

Colin Hart, Director of the Christian Institute, comments: 'Women want a lower abortion limit, and MPs should think carefully before ignoring their views on this sensitive issue.

'When told of actual survival rates of babies born before 24 weeks people back a lower abortion limit. Three in four women also want a limit of 20 weeks or lower to be more in line with other EU countries.'

Polling details

ComRes interviewed 1,014 GB adults by telephone between 2 and 4 May 2008. Data were weighted to be representative demographically of all GB adults. ComRes is a member of the British Polling Council and abides by its rules. See www.comres.co.uk
16 May 2008

⇨ The above information is reprinted with kind permission from the Christian Institute. Visit www.christian.org.uk for more information.

© *Christian Institute*

Abortion laws – right or wrong?

Do you agree or disagree with the following statement? 'Women who are considering whether to have an abortion should be given a statutory legal right to be told of all the physical and psychological risks known to be associated with it.' Results by gender.

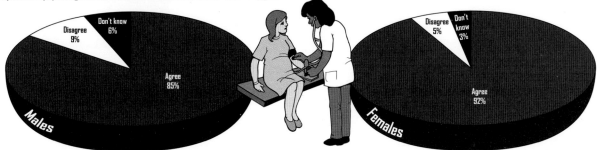

Males: Disagree 9%, Don't know 6%, Agree 85%

Females: Disagree 5%, Don't know 3%, Agree 92%

In the last year for which figures are available, government statistics show that 52 babies survived having been born earlier than 24 weeks. At one specialist neo-natal unit in Britain, five out of seven babies born at 22 weeks' gestation survived. In light of this, do you think that the upper time limit for abortion should be kept at 24 weeks, increased, or decreased? Results by age group.

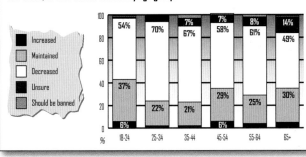

	18-24	25-34	35-44	45-54	55-64	65+
Increased		7%	7%		8%	14%
Maintained	54%	70%	67%	58%	61%	49%
Decreased	37%	22%	21%	29%	25%	30%
Unsure / Should be banned	6%			6%		

In Great Britain the upper time limit for abortion is 24 weeks. By comparison, in most other EU countries the limit is 12 weeks or lower. In light of this difference, what do you think the limit should be in Britain?

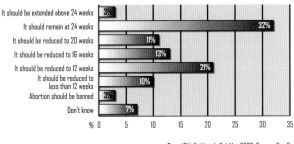

	%
It should be extended above 24 weeks	3%
It should remain at 24 weeks	32%
It should be reduced to 20 weeks	11%
It should be reduced to 16 weeks	13%
It should be reduced to 12 weeks	21%
It should be reduced to less than 12 weeks	10%
Abortion should be banned	3%
Don't know	7%

Base: 1014. Fieldwork: 2-4 May 2008. Source: ComRes.

Public support for early abortion laws

A majority of the public would like a change in the law to allow a woman to choose early abortion and they accept later abortions

Doctors for a Woman's Choice on Abortion celebrate quietly with millions of women and their families on Sunday 27 April, the 40th anniversary of the implementation of the 1967 Abortion Act, arguably one of the most successful public health measures in the last century.

82% agreed that a woman should be able to have an abortion up to 24 weeks if she had been a victim of rape and 78% agreed that this was justified if the woman's health was at risk

DWCA is releasing for the first time an opinion poll which asked some new questions. Firstly, whether respondents thought that 'the law should be changed to provide a woman with the right to choose to have an abortion within the first 12 weeks of pregnancy after consultation with a doctor'. Of those who answered this question, 81% agreed with such a change in the law.

It is regrettable that another attack on the abortion law is expected in this Parliamentary session when the Human Fertilisation and Embryology Bill returns to the Commons. Anti-abortion MPs are expected to try to reduce the upper time limit from 24 weeks to 20 weeks, but the DWCA poll indicates that when given some of the reasons women may present late, a majority of the public accept the need for abortions up to 24 weeks.

82% agreed that a woman should be able to have an abortion up to 24 weeks if she had been a victim of rape and 78% agreed that this was justified if the woman's health was at risk, with only 11% being opposed. A smaller majority, 53%, agreed that 'if a woman's partner became increasingly violent as the pregnancy progressed' she should be able to have an abortion up to 24 weeks and 26% were opposed to this.

We hope that MPs will take note of these findings and resist calls to restrict the law, which needs liberalising to bring it in line with many other European countries who passed their laws after 1967.

Professor Colin Francome and Professor Wendy Savage of Middlesex University designed the questions and DWCA funded the poll.
27 April 2008

⇨ The above information is re-printed with kind permission from DWCA (Doctors for a Woman's Choice on Abortion). Visit www.dwca.org for more information.
© DWCA

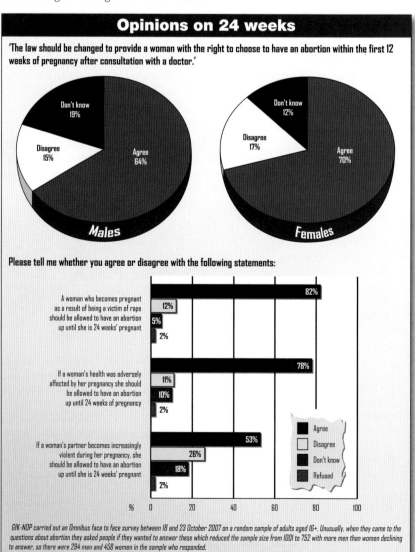

Opinions on 24 weeks

'The law should be changed to provide a woman with the right to choose to have an abortion within the first 12 weeks of pregnancy after consultation with a doctor.'

Males:
- Don't know 19%
- Disagree 15%
- Agree 64%

Females:
- Don't know 12%
- Disagree 17%
- Agree 70%

Please tell me whether you agree or disagree with the following statements:

A woman who becomes pregnant as a result of being a victim of rape should be allowed to have an abortion up until she is 24 weeks' pregnant
- 82%
- 12%
- 5%
- 2%

If a woman's health was adversely affected by her pregnancy she should be allowed to have an abortion up until 24 weeks of pregnancy
- 78%
- 11%
- 10%
- 2%

If a woman's partner becomes increasingly violent during her pregnancy, she should be allowed to have an abortion up until she is 24 weeks' pregnant
- 53%
- 26%
- 18%
- 2%

Legend:
- Agree
- Disagree
- Don't know
- Refused

% 0   20   40   60   80   100

GfK-NOP carried out an Omnibus face to face survey between 18 and 23 October 2007 on a random sample of adults aged 16+. Unusually, when they came to the questions about abortion they asked people if they wanted to answer these which reduced the sample size from 1001 to 752 with more men than women declining to answer, so there were 294 men and 458 women in the sample who responded.

Source: DWCA (Doctors for a Woman's Choice on Abortion)

20 reasons to cut the abortion limit

Information from The 20 Weeks Campaign

There are around 200,000 abortions per year in Britain, 600 per day. By law babies can be aborted up to 24 weeks. The Human Fertilisation and Embryology Bill currently in the House of Commons will allow MPs to change this outdated law. We want to cut the limit to 20 weeks or below.

1 Public, parliamentary and medical opinion is changing on late abortion. 63% of MPs, two-thirds of GPs, nearly two-thirds of the public and more than three-quarters of women support a reduction in the 24-week upper age limit.

2 High-profile cases of babies surviving well below 24 weeks, like Manchester's Millie McDonagh, born at 22 weeks, and the world's most premature baby, Amillia Taylor, who was born a week younger, both in October 2006.

3 High-resolution 3D ultrasound images, pioneered by Professor Stuart Campbell, have shown babies in amazing detail 'walking', yawning, stretching and sucking their thumbs in the womb.

4 In top neo-natal units, such as in Minneapolis, Minnesota, 80% of babies born at 24 weeks and 66% of babies born at 23 weeks will survive. Recent figures from University College London are similar.

5 Recent research, such as that by Professor Sunny Anand from the University of Arkansas, has shown that fetuses are well enough developed to feel pain down to 18 weeks' gestation.

6 Mothers first feel their babies kick at 19 weeks in a first pregnancy and at 17 weeks in a later pregnancy.

7 Stories of babies born alive after botched abortions, as young as 16 weeks, are increasingly common and have understandably shocked the public.

8 The number of abortions carried out between 20 and 24 weeks has been rising in recent years. Lowering the limit to 20 weeks for normal babies will save almost 2,300 young lives per year.

9 Leading public figures including Opposition leader David Cameron are calling for a cut to at least 20 weeks.

Britain has the most liberal abortion laws in Europe

---

10 Britain has the most liberal abortion laws in Europe. A termination can be obtained up to 24 weeks of pregnancy – double the limits in France and Germany and six weeks' later than in Sweden or Norway.

11 The methods required to abort a post-20-week baby are abhorrent. To avoid a live birth a lethal injection is given into the baby's heart through the mother's abdominal wall. The baby is then delivered stillborn or is surgically dismembered and removed from the uterus limb by limb.

12 A recent Royal College of Psychiatrists report acknowledges a link between abortion and mental illness. This is worse with late abortions, especially those for fetal abnormality.

13 The vast majority of late abortions (after 16 weeks) take place in private clinics but are classified as 'NHS Agency' (ie charged to the NHS). Abortions over 20 weeks cost from £1,300 to £1,600 each and there are inevitably financial vested interests involved.

14 Babies are now undergoing surgery in the womb under 24 weeks. The photograph of Samuel Armas having surgery at 21 weeks for spina bifida has received international attention.

15 Very few, if any, UK graduates are now willing to perform abortions beyond 16 weeks. Almost all doctors performing late abortions in the UK in BPAS clinics are from overseas.

16 A Royal College of Obstetricians and Gynaecologists (RCOG) guideline, supporting an upper limit of 24 weeks, was published in 2004 and needs to be updated in line with the latest evidence on fetal sentience, ultrasound and neo-natal survival.

17 The British Medical Association's opposition to lowering the limit is not supported by the majority of its members and almost 1,000 BMA members recently signed a petition against attempts to further liberalise BMA policy.

18 Pregnancy testing kits are freely available at chemists and there is now little excuse for not diagnosing pregnancy long before 20 weeks.

19 The House of Commons Science and Technology Committee's report recommending retention of the 24-week upper limit was heavily influenced by pro-abortion witnesses.

20
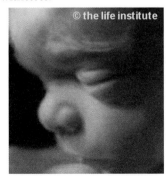
© the life institute

⇨ The above information is reprinted with kind permission from The 20 Weeks Campaign. Visit www.the20weekscampaign.org for more.

© The 20 Weeks Campaign

24 reasons for 24 weeks

Information from the Pro Choice Forum

By Jennie Bristow

The Tory MP turned anti-abortion campaigner Nadine Dorries on 6 May launched her latest publicity stunt: a website detailing 20 reasons for reducing the upper time limit for abortion from 24 weeks' gestation to 20 weeks. In fact, this amounts to one reason: that Dorries does not approve of abortion, and she wants to stop women from having them.

There are any number of reasons why the time limit for abortion should not be lowered, and these too come down to one overriding argument. In order to play a full and equal role in society, women need the ability to control their fertility, and without access to abortion they cannot do that. Politicians understood this 41 years ago when they passed the Abortion Act, and they understand it now.

As Parliament moves to discuss amendments to the abortion law through the Human Fertilisation and Embryology Bill, those of us committed to women's rights and freedom should counter the spurious arguments and junk science put forward by Nadine Dorries and the anti-abortion lobby, by offering a steady stream of reason, compassion and sound evidence. Here are 24 ways to start.

1) Women need access to safe, legal abortion

History tells us that women with unwanted pregnancies will try their best to end them, sometimes with severe risk to their health. The 1967 Abortion Act was a humane piece of legislation, borne out of the understanding that women need and deserve to control their fertility, not be penalised because of it.

2) There is no right number of abortions

Nadine Dorries' campaign cautions that there are 200,000 abortions per year in Britain, and that it is 'time to slow down'. But what is the right number of abortions for anti-abortion activists? 100,000, 100, 1? For the anti-abortion movement to haggle over what might be a more acceptable number of abortions is as nonsensical a stance as it is unprincipled.

3) There is no right time to have an abortion

Women never set out to have abortions – they are always the least bad option at a difficult time. While earlier abortions are easier, safer and less unpleasant than those in later gestations, there are a multitude of reasons why women may not have accessed abortion earlier on. None of these make that woman's abortion any less necessary, or her any less deserving of it. Women need abortions when they need them, not when somebody else thinks is the right time to have them.

4) Women should not be pushed or panicked into having abortions before they have made their decision

Developments in early abortion techniques and provision are progressive because they expand choice for women, giving women seeking abortion the option of having it sooner rather than later. A reduction in the time limit would reduce choice, and risk pushing women who are agonising over whether to continue their pregnancy into making a decision to terminate it before they have definitely decided that that is what they want to do – as well as forcing other women to continue an unwanted pregnancy to term.

5) There is no right reason to have an abortion

Among the many reasons cited by women why they had an abortion in the second trimester of pregnancy, a 2007 study found that 'I was not sure about having the abortion, and it took me a while to make my mind up and ask for one' emerged as an important reason. Women can be deeply ambivalent about their pregnancies, and think very carefully before seeking abortion. Research shows that women do not take their abortion decisions lightly, and that these are personal decisions based on complex circumstances that policy cannot even begin to prescribe.

6) Women often make their abortion decisions based on their desire to be good parents

It is a common misconception that women seeking abortion do not want children. Yet almost half (47%) of women who had abortions in England and Wales in 2006 had had one or more previous pregnancies that resulted in a live or stillbirth. Research shows that an important factor in women's decision-making about abortion is how well able they feel to be a good parent to a baby, or another baby, in the context of their particular family circumstances. In a social context where there is a great deal of pressure to take parenting very seriously, why should women be penalised for understanding that they cannot do that at this moment in time?

7) Changes in women's circumstances can mean that a wanted pregnancy becomes unwanted

Women who have wanted to be pregnant, or reconciled themselves to pregnancy, may find themselves seeking abortion when something in their lives goes badly wrong: the death or desertion of a partner, the discovery of fetal abnormality, or a major change in financial or other personal circumstances, to name a few reasons. For these women, the option not to have to go through with a pregnancy conceived in very different circumstances is crucial to retaining their reproductive autonomy and some control over their lives. To be told that they are 'too late' on the basis of spurious arguments advanced by the anti-abortion movement is insensitive and inhumane.

8) Women can take several months to realise they are pregnant

Contraceptive failure, irregular periods or continuing periods are just some of the reasons why a woman might take several weeks or months to suspect that she is pregnant. Women who believe that there is no way they could be pregnant are not going to be looking out for the signs, and at the point at which a woman realises she is pregnant the gestation may be quite advanced. In the absence of other reasons to reduce the upper limit, why should these women be penalised?

9) Women can be let down by contraception

Access to abortion exists as an integral part of reproductive health policy because it is understood that contraception fails. People sometimes fail to use it properly, and at other times it fails. The argument that 'there is no excuse' for unintended pregnancy at a time when contraception is readily available fails to grasp the essential point that contraceptive access provides no guarantees without the availability of abortion as a back-up.

10) Women know that they are carrying a human fetus well before there are photos to prove it

The last of Nadine Dorries' '20 reasons for 20 weeks' is a picture of a fetus looking like a baby. She might want to ask herself, what do pregnant women think they are carrying: an alien, a baby frog? Women seeking abortion are fully aware that if they continue the pregnancy, they will give birth to a human baby; and it is precisely because of the consequences of having and raising a child that they have reached the decision to have an abortion.

11) Unwanted children carry a significant physical, emotional and financial cost

Women know that having a child is a life-changing event, and that pregnancy is a major physical undertaking. While women pregnant with wanted children often welcome this, those for whom a child is unwanted face far more than a minor inconvenience through being forced to carry a pregnancy to term.

Almost half (47%) of women who had abortions in England and Wales in 2006 had had one or more previous pregnancies that resulted in a live or stillbirth

---

12) Women's mental health does not suffer as a result of abortion

Despite persistent claims from the anti-abortion movement that abortion causes mental illness, evidence does not show a causal link between abortion and negative mental health. While some women have serious psychological problems following abortion, these cases are relatively rare, and they are often a continuation of problems a woman has experienced before. Research does indicate that the most stressful and emotionally difficult time for women is immediately before the abortion, when they are making the decision to terminate. Post-abortion, the most common response exhibited by women is relief.

13) Women's physical health does not suffer as a result of abortion

Legal abortion carried out by trained practitioners is now a very safe, effective procedure. A woman is more likely to die as a result of pregnancy and childbirth than from terminating a pregnancy. Despite claims to the contrary by the anti-abortion lobby, there is no proven association between abortion and ectopic pregnancy, infertility or breast cancer. As with all clinical procedures, there is a small risk of complications following abortion – but women who undergo the procedure do so having weighed potential problems against the definite and known disadvantages of having an unwanted child.

14) Women's access to abortion services is often not as rapid as it could be

Access to abortion in the UK has improved greatly in recent years, but it continues to take time to arrange an abortion – particularly at later gestations, where fewer services are available and the procedure demands greater resources. It is already the case that a woman seeking abortion at 21 weeks may find herself pushed over the 24-week limit by service constraints. Reducing the time limit further would exacerbate this problem.

15) There is no evidence of improved fetal viability prior to 24 weeks

In its recent inquiry into 'Scientific Developments Relating to the

Abortion Act 1967', the Parliamentary Science and Technology Committee (STC) found that while survival rates (viability) at 24 weeks and over have improved since 1990, viability has not improved below that gestational point. This point has been reinforced by recent British studies. The STC concluded that there is no scientific basis, on the grounds of viability, to reduce the upper time limit on abortion – a point accepted by the government.

16) There is no evidence that fetuses feel pain before 24 weeks

The STC's review of the evidence also found while fetuses have physiological reactions to stimuli, this does not indicate that pain is consciously felt, especially not below 24 weeks. It further concluded that these factors may be relevant to clinical practice but do not appear to be relevant to the question of abortion law.

17) 4D images tells us nothing of relevance to abortion

The anti-abortion lobby has made much of the advances in 4D ultrasound technology, in which fetuses appear to be 'walking' in the womb. But while these make for emotive images, scientific opinion has stressed that they contain no insights into fetal sentience or viability.

18) A 20-week limit would make very little difference to the abortion statistics, and a massive difference to the minority of individual women whom it would affect

A tiny proportion of abortions in England and Wales are performed at 20-24 weeks gestation: fewer than 3,000 abortions, comprising 1.5% of the total number. This figure has remained stable over the past decade despite policy attempts to encourage abortion at earlier gestations, indicating that women's reasons for later abortions are more complex than simply struggling to access services earlier on. Reducing Dorries' headline figure of '200,000 abortions per year' by 3,000 would do nothing to 'slow down' the national abortion statistics, but would force hundreds of individual woman to bear an unwanted child.

19) '20 weeks' is an arbitrary figure

If there is no evidence of improved

fetal viability at any gestation under 24 weeks, why pick 20 weeks as a cut-off point? Why not 22, or 18, or 10, or none? The focus on '20 weeks' shows how little scientific basis there is for this campaign, despite its pretensions.

20) '20 reasons for 20 weeks' is a dishonest campaign

The anti-abortion lobby is opposed to all abortions, but it knows that the public is not. By focusing on emotive, later abortions, anti-abortion campaigners pretend that there are legitimate reasons to ban these abortions while allowing abortion at earlier gestations to continue. There are no such legitimate reasons; and for campaigners to claim that there are is cowardly and dishonest.

21) Public opinion accepts that women need access to abortion

An Ipsos MORI poll carried out in 2006 found that 63% of adults in the UK agreed that 'if a woman wants an abortion, she should not have to continue with her pregnancy', while only 18% disagreed. There is no public movement to ban abortion, or even to restrict it further. While nobody likes abortion, the public accepts that it is a necessary fact of life in a country committed to women's equality and reproductive freedom.

22) Political opinion accepts that women need access to abortion

The 1967 Abortion Act was conceived as a necessary public health initiative, and as a progressive piece of legislation that would enable women to play a full role in public life. Since that time, Parliament has shown no desire to repeal this legislation, and the government today remains committed to providing women with access to safe, legal abortion. The government has accepted that there is no scientific case for a reduction in the upper time limit, and it is to be hoped that it will retain a principled commitment to allowing women access to abortions when they need them, not when the odd pro-life MP claims they ought to have them.

23) Medical opinion accepts that women need access to abortion

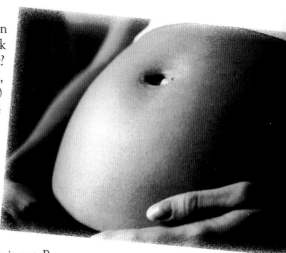

The British Medical Association has called upon MPs to vote against any attempt to reduce the 24-week time limit, on the grounds that there is no 'scientific justification' for such a move. Because the law requires two doctors to permit any woman to have an abortion, the medical profession is an important player in both abortion policy and practice: that it sees no grounds for reducing the time limit for abortion is a serious consideration.

24) Women's lives are too important to be played with by political poseurs

Since the start of her one-woman anti-abortion campaign in Parliament two years ago, Nadine Dorries MP has shown herself to be ignorant of the evidence about abortion, insensitive about women seeking abortion, and willing to play fast and loose with the facts according to whatever might suit her latest campaign slogan. Women seeking abortion are making decisions about a highly personal issue, which they are attempting to deal with in the best practical way they know. They should not be used as pawns in a game of political point-scoring, but provided with the progressive law and effective service that a civilised society should demand.

Jennie Bristow is editor of the BPAS journal Abortion Review, *and writes* spiked's *monthly 'Guide to Subversive Parenting'.*

⇨ The above information is reprinted with kind permission from the Pro Choice Forum. Visit www.prochoiceforum.org.uk for more or to view references for this article.

© Pro Choice Forum

Women perform 'DIY abortions' with online pills

Chilling Internet drug market nothing more than modern version of backstreet abortion, says Alive and Kicking

A BJOG article published today assesses the effects on 400 women who accessed abortion drugs on the Internet. Major players in this grisly market are the same group (Women on Waves) who sailed the seas offering offshore terminations in their specially-equipped abortion ship.

'When taking the life of the unborn child becomes so trivialised that women are encouraged to buy the abortion drugs through the Internet and perform DIY abortions at home, we have to ask ourselves if society has descended into a complete moral void,' said a spokesperson for the campaign group Alive and Kicking.

'Abortion, whether by drugs or surgery, whether early or late in pregnancy, always ends a human life and this is certainly our primary reaction to this latest news.

'But we need to focus clearly on the welfare of women as well, and note that the BJOG journal records that 11% of the women who availed themselves of the do-it-yourself abortion drugs required later medical intervention. This underlines the physical dangers to women inherent in this method. Without medical assistance, without correct appraisal of the general health of the mother (including her age), without proper confirmation of the gestational age of her developing child, it is inevitable that the tragedies will increase.

'The other significant aspect of abortion is the effect it has on the mental health of women, which will never be addressed properly with this latest cynical development. Women facing unplanned pregnancy are particularly vulnerable, and need careful counselling, care and support. Quick-fix Internet abortion makes no provision even for reliably identifying 'clients', let alone addressing their psychological health or determining whether they are being coerced.

'Some of the medical details the website does highlight are unlikely to be verified by a young girl or vulnerable impoverished woman desperately trying to hide an unwanted pregnancy. Such clients are unlikely to go for ultrasound diagnosis, be aware of the risks of ectopic pregnancy, know for sure how pregnant they are, or have any idea as to how the abortion might affect future pregnancies. Nor are they likely to have ready access to medical help should things go wrong.

'Alive & Kicking was horrified to find through the same sources online advice to women explaining how to try and put the abortion drugs together by subterfuge. Here, for example, are some recommendations as to how to obtain misoprostol, a drug in mainstream medicine developed for gastric ulcer treatment and as an adjunct in rheumatoid arthritis, but which can on its own bring about abortion:

⇨ tell the pharmacist 'that your grandmother has rheumatoid arthritis';
⇨ try 'the black market (places where you can also buy Marijuana)';
⇨ ask somebody else to persuade the pharmacist to provide the drug; 'a male friend might have fewer problems' in doing this.

'Note that the drug dosages vary considerably between the various drugs containing misoprostol (25mg, 50mg, 75mg or 200mg). Women are expected to make their own calculations as to correct usage; again unlikely when they are reacting in a crisis.

'This is nothing more than a modern version of backstreet abortion. It is time for the pro-abortion lobby to wake up and recognise that women deserve much better than abortion, and that the only caring way forward is to come up with real solutions to unplanned pregnancy which do not involve killing the unborn child and harming the woman.'
11 July 2008

⇨ The above information is reprinted with kind permission from Alive and Kicking. Visit www.aliveandkickingcampaign.org for more information.

© *Alive and Kicking*

Now, let's see... www.dodgydoityourselfabortions.com

Easy access to abortion makes sense

A website offering abortions by post has caused uproar. But this is a service that has the potential to save women's lives

By Angela Phillips

Till now pornographers have been the biggest single gainers from the existence of the Internet, so today's news that an international feminist organisation is using the same facility to provide a free abortion service to women in countries where termination of pregnancy is restricted feels like an important correction.

The Women on Web service provides safe abortion medication for a donation, or for free to those who cannot afford to donate. It also provides a follow-up and support service. Of course, no abortion method is 100% safe. A British Journal of Obstetrics review of the service found that 11% had needed a follow-up surgical procedure but, as Women on Web points out, given that every seven minutes a woman somewhere in the world dies from a botched illegal procedure, an almost 90% chance of a safe, effective abortion has got to be a very big improvement.

Of course there will be those who are shocked and horrified and indeed the Today Programme this morning concentrated almost entirely on the so called 'moral' and 'ethical' question of women using a website to get around national legislation outlawing abortion.

There is something unbearably smug about hearing men chatter on about how the really important thing to focus on is avoiding pregnancy and that there is not enough discussion of this aspect of fertility. Good grief, where have these men been all their lives? Have they any idea just how much time women spend worrying about that very question? Do they really think that the average woman having unprotected sex is swept away in ecstasy – and not secretly wondering if she will get away with it this time?

To most women abortion is not a matter of morality but of practicality. It is the norm in developed societies to have not more than two children, and yet we have up to 35 years of healthy reproductive life. We all do what we can to stick to the norm – but inevitably accidents happen. It's like driving. You have a clean license for years and then, bang, you are holed by a bollard. (It might not be quite like that, but every woman reading this will know what I mean).

To me, the only ethical and moral issue is that governments who are indirectly responsible for the deaths of thousands of women every year are not asked about their own 'morality' and ethics. Is it ethical for any government to deny women access to a safe back-up arrangement when accidents happen? Forcing a woman to have a baby she doesn't want is not moral or ethical. It's not moral or ethical to bring babies into the world who are not wanted and may not be loved.

11 July 2008

© Guardian Newspapers Limited 2008

Teachers asked for advice about abortion

Information from Abortion Review

A poll carried out for Teachers TV finds that teachers think information about abortion should be given in school.

A poll of more than 800 people working in education found that the majority (67%) think information about abortion should be included in sex education classes. But 82% believe discussing the topic could offend parents, and 42% think it could offend students.

In total 24% of secondary school teachers who responded to the poll said they had been asked for advice on abortion.

When asked about the reasons for Britain's high rate of teenage pregnancy, 42% of those polled blamed the breakdown of values in society.

Almost a fifth, 19%, said it was because of the sexualisation of young people and children and 16% blamed sex education.

'It has been 40 years since the legalisation of abortion in this country but it appears that, for the education workforce, the topic still needs to be handled sensitively to avoid causing offence to students and their parents,' Andrew Bethell, chief executive of Teachers TV, said.

The poll was published to mark a week of programming dedicated to sex and relationships on the channel.

25 January 2009

⇨ The above information is reprinted with kind permission from Abortion Review, a professional journal produced by the British Pregnancy Advisory Service (BPAS). Visit www.bpas.org for more information.

© British Pregnancy Advisory Service (BPAS)

Shock tactics

Anti-abortion campaigners are being allowed into schools to present their arguments to teenagers, and are making converts. But what about the facts? Kate Hilpern reports

Rawnie Chapman-Kitchin, 15, was aghast when her teacher compared abortion to Nazism, saying that in time history would view both with the same revulsion. 'I'd been expecting a regular RE class, but a different teacher was called in to do a talk called Abortion is Murder,' she says. 'He showed horrifying pictures of dead foetuses, but there was no opportunity to opt out. It was very much a case of "this is the way you need to think".

'One person put their hand up at the end and said, "You've changed my mind. I thought abortion was OK, but now I don't." Others agreed and still hold those views. But I've since found out that some of what the teacher was saying isn't even true – for example, about how they do abortions.'

Anti-abortion presentations in schools are not a one-off. At the beginning of this term, the Society for the Protection of the Unborn Child (Spuc) wrote to every secondary school in the country to offer its PowerPoint presentation. Katherine Hampton, education officer at Spuc, says she visits around 10 schools a term and supervises a further 40 trained speakers across the country. The organisation Life delivered 816 school talks during 2006-07 through its 'active schools department', reaching 37,803 students across 316 schools – a 20% increase on the previous year. Then there are the individual teachers, like Rawnie's, who offer to air their anti-choice views to classes. Having realised that teenagers are the most susceptible to anti-abortion messages, lobbyists are increasingly targeting 13- to 17-year-olds.

While each has differing tactics (for instance, Life doesn't use images), what they all share is an approach to abortion that is highly subjective. What's more, they stand accused of presenting information that is at best questionable and at worst incorrect. Spuc, for

example, tells teenagers there are links between abortion and breast cancer, although organisations such as Cancer Research UK and Breakthrough Breast Cancer have consistently presented research to prove there is no link. The Royal College of Obstetricians and Gynaecologists (RCOG) categorically states that abortion is not associated with an increase in breast-cancer risk. Life says it tells pupils that, although abortion is becoming safer, there are studies that have shown an increased risk of infertility. The RCOG states that there are no proven associations.

Why do schools allow these speakers in? Three reasons. First, they feel they ought to cover abortion but, given its contentious nature, are anxious about how to approach it. An offer from a so-called specialist organisation can come as something of a relief. Second, abortion usually sits within RE, where it is covered as a moral issue, so teachers often welcome the idea of visiting speakers with a strong view. Third, schools like outside speakers – it shows they are widening their pool of educators.

The anti-choice lobby has reason to celebrate. A recent YouGov poll found that only 29% of 17-year-olds were strongly pro-choice. The remainder are either negative or ambivalent, and although it was a small survey, most people in the field agree the

figure sounds about right. The UK Life League – the most hardcore of all the anti-abortion groups – claims it has never had so much support from teenage girls. 'We've noticed a massive difference in the last three years alone. Whereas they used to be largely unreceptive, they now tell us how pleased they are about the work we're doing. I'm not sure what's different, but I wish I could have bottled it up 30 years ago,' says Jim Dowson, its national coordinator.

Samantha Bracey, Rawnie's mother, is amazed that more parents, and schools, are not taking a stand. 'I was really concerned when my daughter told me about the disturbing images she was shown, and even more so when I discovered she'd been told abortions were carried out via caesarean section [called hysterotomy abortions], which isn't true. The teacher consistently referred to the embryo or foetus – medically recognised terms – as a baby, and claimed that pro-abortionists did not use the term "baby" as it was too emotive.'

When Bracey approached the school – Chapel-en-le-Frith High School in Derbyshire – she was assured that, in future, pro-choice opinions would be explored within the class. 'But the teacher who gave the talk still said his intention would be to win his argument, which seems to me to be

missing the purpose of education,' she says. 'Surely issues like abortion should be addressed in a way that makes all the facts available, rather than merely opinion, thus enabling the students to reach a conclusion by informed debate. When it comes to abortion, it's so important – it can affect the rest of their lives.'

Stating the facts

Only one organisation, Education For Choice (EfC), gives pro-choice talks in schools, but with a fraction of the funding and staffing that Spuc and Life enjoy, the number of pupils it reaches is minimal. Lisa Hallgarten, EfC's head of policy and communications, says: 'We don't go in and say you should always have an abortion under every circumstance, which would be the opposite of what they say. We say, here are the facts and it's absolutely your decision.' If someone comes into the classroom believing abortion is murder and leaves still believing that, Hallgarten does not consider it failure. 'That's not our mission. But if someone walks in believing that abortion makes you infertile and they leave with that view, then that would be failure.'

What's needed, she believes, is for schools to move away from presenting the issue as a dichotomy: abortion – is it right or wrong? 'That's so often how it's addressed in schools, which completely ignores the sexual health aspect. Far more productive is exploring how women get into the situation where they consider abortion. Could they have avoided the unwanted pregnancy? And are there situations where it is unavoidable – for example, where contraception fails? Then you can move on to talk about people's different values, at which point we explore some of the reasons people are against abortion as well as reasons why others find it acceptable.'

Like many teachers, Stuart Ash, headteacher at Chapel-en-le-Frith High School, had never heard of EfC. 'We would like nothing more than to present objective, balanced information to our young people. But we found it hard to find any such resource material available for schools and appropriate for the GCSE age range,' he says. 'People say, "Why not look on the Internet?" There's certainly plenty of material there, but you don't know who's behind it. That's why we offered a lesson with the "against" argument and a few weeks later the other side of the coin – although, with hindsight, we feel that time permitting, it would be better to explore both sets of views within the same lesson.' He adds that the lesson attended by Rawnie was prefaced with a statement that the teacher's standpoint was only one of a range of views.

Hallgarten says it is the mis-information presented to pupils that most infuriates her, in particular what she calls the 'huge propaganda machine' around post-abortion trauma. 'There is no evidence that abortion *per se* causes trauma, yet it has been the most effective propaganda tool that has helped much of the anti-abortion movement move from a blame culture (how can you murder your baby?) to women as victims (you poor thing, you'll be terribly traumatised if you have one).'

Many anti-abortion organisations refer to 'post-abortion syndrome', whose symptoms can include panic attacks, relationship problems, self-harm, drug and alcohol abuse, and depression. In fact, it is not a recognised medical condition. In August, the American Psychological Association concluded: 'There is no credible evidence that single elective abortion of an unwanted pregnancy in and of itself causes mental health problems for adult women.'

When it comes to imagery, anti-abortion organisations appear to have two tactics. 'Some organisations use compelling images of happy-looking faces in the womb, which are without doubt beautiful,' says Hallgarten. 'But many claims are made that they are doing things, like smiling, that in fact they can't do until after they are born. Another tactic used in schools is to show a photograph of a foetus at, say, 24 weeks, and then talk about an abortion at 12 weeks. It's all about implication. Then there's the purported pictures of foetal parts in buckets, which is obviously distressing and can have a big impact.'

Spuc opts for both types of pictures. Having watched its presentation, labelled 'standard abortion talk 2008',

I am not surprised to hear that in one class of 16- and 17-year-olds shown the presentation in July, half the students left distressed and some were physically sick.

'The presentation I am going to show you today will give you the information about abortion that we believe everyone should know,' it starts. 'You will see seven pictures showing the development of the baby and four pictures showing the different methods of abortion. The abortion pictures are not very pleasant to look at, and I will warn you before I show them. My intention is not to shock you, rather to inform you sensitively of the truth and reality of what abortion entails.'

I was shocked. Having built up a sentimental picture of the first weeks of foetal development, the first of the abortion images is brutal and bloody, showing a foetus being pulled by its legs out of a woman's cut-open stomach. The method claims to be a hysterotomy abortion – one that is so rarely employed (and only ever used when no other method is safe for the woman) that statistics are not collected on it in the UK. In the US, it is estimated at less than a tenth of 1% of abortions. Spuc says that while some speakers have dropped this image from their talk, others have not.

Another picture shows a premature baby called Kelly and is accompanied by the statement that: 'As long ago as 1985, a study by RCOG said that 72% of babies born between 20 and 25 weeks survived, yet the laws in our country allow unborn babies the same age as Kelly to be aborted.' Spuc says it tells teenagers that the figure is probably far higher today. The actual figures from the 2000 EPICure study into the survival of extremely premature infants, which the RCOG cites and is the best source of information on this topic, says 33% of babies born at 24 weeks, 19.9% at 23 weeks, and 9.1% at 22 weeks live long enough to be discharged from hospital.

Hampton believes that, among young women, the tide is turning towards anti-abortion and likes to think that Spuc has been influential. But she insists its intention is simply 'to leave people with factual information that they can think about', and adds that images are only used with the permission of the teacher, which is given in about 50% of cases.

Samantha Crozier, an RE teacher, was one who gave permission. 'I told Spuc the talk would be to 16-year-olds and that I didn't want them to show anything too graphic, and they said that was fine. Yet the images the presenter used were so shocking that one teacher walked out and another felt she had to turn her back to the class. Many of the students also turned away, while a few left the room and a couple even went home because they were so upset. We had to bring all the students who remained together afterwards and apologise. As far as I'm concerned, it wasn't a case of those pictures not being appropriate for that age group – they're not appropriate for any age group. There was a question of things being outdated, too. One of the images they used was from 1978 and some of the procedures they talked about aren't even used today.'

Life has a different approach, says its education officer, Michaela Aston. 'We want young people to think for themselves. We're not going to tell them what to think. Of course, it would be lovely if they're pro-life, but if they're not that's fine.'

Logical position?

Life's main bugbear appears to be that most people assume abortion is 'perfectly fine' because it's legal. 'That's the general perception. But really we don't want kids to inherit these views. We want them to think about the principles they live by, what values are important to them. We never show any horrid pictures, ever, as a matter of policy. And we look at all the arguments for and against so that they engage with the debate,' says Aston. It sounds reasonably unbiased, but Aston believes – as every member of Life does – 'that because we believe human life begins at the moment of fertilisation, then the pro-life position is the only logical position to take'.

Although not explicitly an anti-abortion organisation, Care Confidential is another piece in the jigsaw. Claiming to offer a neutral service, 'which helps teenagers think through what options are available to them and how they might feel about those options when faced with a crisis',

the charity provides talks in schools. A bit of digging turns up some significant issues. First, Care Confidential is run by the charity Christian Action Research and Education (Care), whose charitable aims, as listed with the Charity Commission, are: 'The advancement and propagation of the Christian Gospel and in particular Christian teachings as it bears on or affects national and individual morality and ethics.' Second, the vast majority of stories from women who have had abortions that it publicises are negative, although it does publish all the stories it receives. And finally, despite research pointing to the significant and lasting psychological damage that can be faced by women who put their babies up for adoption, Care Confidential encourages young women to consider adoption as a positive alternative. Care Confidential declined to make any comment for this article.

Religious bias

Dr Geraldine Brady, research fellow at Coventry University, says she has come across organisations that play down their anti-abortion agenda by presenting themselves as neutral. 'One of them [not Care Confidential] was Christian-based, employing professionally-trained counsellors. However, it transpired that the religion did seep through, and some of the literature they were providing to schools revealed that quite clearly. They were going into schools to educate young people about the facts around termination, foetal

development, abortion procedures, but with the literature that was used and the way it was used, it became obvious that an anti-abortion stance was coming through.'

Research shows that even where pro-choice groups have been invited into schools to 'balance' the picture, it can be too late. 'We found people from pro-choice groups in this situation felt they were up against it, having been cast in a negative light,' says Brady.

Ann Furedi, chief executive of the British Pregnancy Advisory Service, believes we should all be concerned about anti-choice organisations accessing young people. 'From their point of view, targeting these particularly impressionable and idealistic people is seen as a tactic. They are well-resourced, sometimes drawing on funding from the US, and they have a real mission.' As a result, she says, and despite the increase in the numbers of young people having abortions, 'there is a growing sense among them that it's ultimately wrong'.

Nobody I spoke to suggested that anti-abortion views should be shielded from young people. But, says Furedi, any discussion in school must be honest and provide accurate, impartial and up-to-date information. 'Better still,' she says, 'let's move it out of the RE room and be much more up front about the fact that one in three women will have an abortion at some time in their lives and that basically, if you're fertile and sexually active, you are at risk of an unwanted pregnancy.'

25 November 2008

Reasons for late abortions

Specific reasons reported for delays by at least 20% of the whole sample.

Reason	%	Reason	%
I was not sure about having the abortion, and it took me a while to make my mind up and ask for one	41%	I had to wait more than five days before I could get a consultation appointment to get the go-ahead for the abortion*	24%
I didn't realise I was pregnant earlier because my periods are irregular	38%	My relationship with my partner broke down/changed	23%
I thought the pregnancy was much less advanced than it was when I asked for the abortion	36%	I was worried about what was involved in having an abortion so it took me a while to ask for one	22%
I wasn't sure what I would do if I were pregnant	32%	I didn't realise I was pregnant earlier because I continued having periods	20%
I didn't realise I was pregnant earlier because I was using contraception	31%	I had to wait more than seven days between the consultation and the appointment for the abortion*	20%
I suspected I was pregnant but I didn't do anything about it until the weeks had gone by	30%	I had to wait over 48 hours for an appointment at my/a doctor's surgery to ask for an abortion	20%
I was worried how my parent(s) would react	26%		

* Adjusted for missed appointments.

Base: 883. Source: 'Second-trimester abortions in England and Wales', University of Southampton, 2007.

⇨ More than nine in ten women have their abortion in the first 13 weeks of pregnancy. However, in the UK, you can legally have an abortion at any time up to your 24th week of pregnancy. (page 1)

⇨ More than 190,000 women have an abortion in England and Wales each year. At least a third of British women will have had an abortion by the time they are 45. (page 1)

⇨ Between 1923 and 1933, 15 per cent of maternal deaths were due to illegal abortion. (page 6)

⇨ The majority of abortions are performed at less than eight weeks' gestation. (page 7)

⇨ 20- to 24-year-olds are the age group most likely to have an abortion. (page 7)

⇨ When presented with a list of potential circumstances, six out of ten (61%) British women aged 18-49 say there are certain circumstances in which they think a woman should have the right to access an abortion between 20 and 24 weeks. (page 8)

⇨ Women who have an abortion are 30 per cent more likely to develop a mental illness, some research suggests. (page 9)

⇨ The APA have concluded that there is 'no credible evidence that a single elective abortion of an unwanted pregnancy in and of itself causes mental health problems for adult women'. (page 9)

⇨ Legal restrictions on abortion do not affect its incidence. For example, the abortion rate is 29 in Africa, where abortion is illegal in many circumstances in most countries, and it is 28 in Europe, where abortion is generally permitted on broad grounds. The lowest rates in the world are in Western and Northern Europe, where abortion is accessible with few restrictions. (page 11)

⇨ Worldwide, 48% of all induced abortions are unsafe. However, in developed regions, nearly all abortions (92%) are safe, whereas in developing countries, more than half (55%) are unsafe. (page 12)

⇨ Nearly two-thirds of Northern Irish people polled (62 per cent) say that abortion should be legal in cases of rape or incest, according to a new survey from fpa in Northern Ireland. (page 16)

⇨ Over a third of all pregnancies, across the world, are unplanned. (page 17)

⇨ 26% of the world's population live in countries where abortion is prohibited. (page 18)

⇨ Some very premature babies can now be kept alive, which has altered ideas about when foetuses become human beings with human rights. The law in England and Wales is based on the fact that after 24 weeks the foetus is often viable, in that with medical assistance it can survive outside the womb. (page 19)

⇨ According to the Safe Mother-hood Initiative, 75 million of the 200 million pregnancies that take place around the world each year are unplanned. (page 19)

⇨ Department of Health data show that 435 children were born after less than 24 weeks of pregnancy during 2005. Of those, 52 survived for at least a year. (page 24)

⇨ The GP Newspaper's survey of 480 UK GPs found a third would refuse to work in a surgery or polyclinic offering abortion, more than half believed offering such abortions would increase the total rate and 61% did not believe practices should be offering such services at all. (page 25)

⇨ A survey by Marie Stopes International of more than 7,000 GPs has shown that 82 per cent describe themselves as 'pro-choice'. (page 26)

⇨ 92 per cent of women (and 89 per cent of the general public) agree that women should have a statutory legal right to be told of all the physical and psychological risks known to be associated with abortion. (page 29)

⇨ 82% of people surveyed agreed that a woman should be able to have an abortion up to 24 weeks if she had been a victim of rape and 78% agreed that this was justified if the woman's health was at risk, with only 11% being opposed. (page 30)

⇨ Almost half (47%) of women who had abortions in England and Wales in 2006 had had one or more previous pregnancies that resulted in a live or stillbirth. (page 33)

⇨ A poll of more than 800 people working in education found that the majority (67%) think information about abortion should be included in sex education classes. But 82% believe discussing the topic could offend parents, and 42% think it could offend students. (page 36)

⇨ A recent YouGov poll found that only 29% of 17-year-olds were strongly pro-choice. The remainder are either negative or ambivalent. (page 37)

GLOSSARY

Abortifacient

A substance or medicine which induces an abortion.

Abortion

The ending of a pregnancy through the death and expulsion of the foetus. It can occur naturally (spontaneous abortion), but this is more commonly referred to as a miscarriage. The deliberate termination of an unwanted pregnancy (induced abortion) is what people are normally referring to when they use the word 'abortion'.

The Abortion Act 1967

This act decriminalised abortion in cases where it had been certified by two doctors that certain grounds had been met, such as a serious risk to the mental or physical health of the pregnant woman.

Backstreet abortion

Before the Abortion Act 1967, it was virtually impossible to procure a legal termination in the UK and some women opted for unsafe, illegal procedures to end their pregnancies, known as backstreet abortions. Procedures could be very dangerous, and many women died.

Contraception

Anything which prevents conception (pregnancy). So-called 'barrier methods' such as condoms work by stopping sperm from reaching an egg during intercourse, and are also effective in protecting against sexually transmitted infections. Hormonal methods such as the contraceptive pill change the way the user's body works to prevent an egg from being fertilised, or in the case of emergency contraception (the 'morning-after pill'), to prevent a fertilised egg from becoming implanted in the womb.

Do-It-Yourself (DIY) abortions

A term coined to describe abortions carried out by women in their own homes using abortifacient drugs (generally procured via the Internet). Women living in countries where abortion is illegal may choose to do this, but taking abortifacients outside a medical setting and without an appropriate assessment can be dangerous.

Embryo

Between day 14 and week eight of pregnancy, the fertilised egg is referred to as an embryo.

Foetus

After the eighth week of pregnancy, an unborn baby is referred to as a foetus.

Gestation

The development period of an embryo or foetus between conception and birth.

Global Gag Rule

Also known as the Mexico City Policy. The so-called 'Global Gag Rule' was first introduced in 1984 and reintroduced by George W. Bush in 2001, before being overturned again by President Obama in 2009. The rule prohibited international sexual health organisations in receipt of US funds from using their own money to provide abortion information, services and care.

Human Fertilisation and Embryology Act 1990

This act amended the 1967 Abortion Act by reducing the maximum time limit for an abortion from 28 to 24 weeks after it was demonstrated that due to medical advances, babies born at 28 weeks and under were capable of survival.

Informed consent

A condition where someone can be said to have given consent to something only upon a full knowledge of the facts surrounding it. In some US states, informed consent or 'right to know' laws require a woman to be given information by her abortion provider about her legal rights, alternatives to abortion (such as adoption) and medical facts before the procedure. Some lobby groups have advocated introducing similar laws in the UK.

Pro-choice

Pro-choice supporters believe that it is a woman's choice whether to have an abortion or not, as it is her body which is affected by the pregnancy. They believe the choice to have an abortion should be available to all.

Pro-life

Pro-life supporters believe that life begins at conception, and that the right of the unborn child to life should be the primary concern when considering the ethics of abortion. They believe the law should be changed so that abortion would be heavily restricted or outlawed in the UK.

Sanctity of life

A term used by people of faith (particularly Christians) to describe the sacred nature of all human life which has been created by God, as they believe, in His image. It is often used in debates relating to abortion, euthanasia and cloning.

Viability

This refers to the capacity of a foetus to survive outside the womb. In UK law, the 24th week of pregnancy is the point at which the foetus is considered to be viable, and therefore the latest point at which an abortion can be performed: however, some people argue that this should be reduced as medical advances mean that some premature babies born at 24 weeks or fewer are surviving.

Additional Resources

Other Issues titles

If you are interested in researching further some of the issues raised in *Abortion – Rights and Ethics*, you may like to read the following titles in the **Issues** series:

⇨ Vol. 174 *Selling Sex* (ISBN 978 1 86168 488 2)

⇨ Vol. 173 *Sexual Health* (ISBN 978 1 86168 487 5)

⇨ Vol. 164 *The AIDS Crisis* (ISBN 978 1 86168 468 4)

⇨ Vol. 152 *Euthanasia and the Right to Die* (ISBN 978 1 86168 439 4)

⇨ Vol. 148 *Religious Beliefs* (ISBN 978 1 86168 421 9)

⇨ Vol. 144 *The Cloning Debate* (ISBN 978 1 86168 410 3)

⇨ Vol. 141 *Mental Health* (ISBN 978 1 86168 407 3)

⇨ Vol. 133 *Teen Pregnancy and Lone Parents* (ISBN 978 1 86168 379 3)

⇨ Vol. 125 *Understanding Depression* (ISBN 978 1 86168 364 9)

⇨ Vol. 124 *Parenting Issues* (ISBN 978 1 86168 363 2)

⇨ Vol. 123 *Young People and Health* (ISBN 978 1 86168 362 5)

For more information about these titles, visit our website at www.independence.co.uk/publicationslist

Useful organisations

You may find the websites of the following organisations useful for further research:

⇨ **The 20 Weeks Campaign:** www.the20weekscampaign.org

⇨ **Abortion Rights:** www.abortionrights.org.uk

⇨ **Alive and Kicking:** www.aliveandkickingcampaign.org

⇨ **Best Health:** http://besthealth.bmj.com

⇨ **British Pregnancy Advisory Service:** www.bpas.org

⇨ **The Christian Institute:** www.christian.org.uk

⇨ **The Christian Medical Fellowship:** www.cmf.org.uk

⇨ **DWCA:** www.dwca.org

⇨ **Education for Choice:** www.efc.org.uk

⇨ **fpa:** www.fpa.org.uk

⇨ **Guttmacher Institute:** www.guttmacher.org

⇨ **International Planned Parenthood Federation:** www.ippf.org

⇨ **Life:** www.lifecharity.org.uk

⇨ **Pro Choice Forum:** www.prochoiceforum.org.uk

⇨ **TheSite:** www.thesite.org

ACKNOWLEDGEMENTS

The publisher is grateful for permission to reproduce the following material.

While every care has been taken to trace and acknowledge copyright, the publisher tenders its apology for any accidental infringement or where copyright has proved untraceable. The publisher would be pleased to come to a suitable arrangement in any such case with the rightful owner.

Chapter One: Terminating a Pregnancy

Having an abortion, © BMJ Group, *Recovering after an abortion*, © TheSite, *History of legal abortion*, © Life, *History of abortion law in the UK*, © Abortion Rights, *Attitudes towards abortion – survey*, © Ipsos MORI, *Abortions linked to mental illness*, © Telegraph Group Ltd, London 2008, *Abortion 'does not cause mental health problems'*, © British Pregnancy Advisory Service, *Facts on induced abortion worldwide*, © Guttmacher Institute, *Obama lifts funds ban for overseas abortion*, © Christian Institute, *'Global Gag Rule' rescinded*, © International Planned Parenthood Federation, *Northern Ireland clarifies when abortion is legal*, © Irish Times 2009, *Public support for abortion in Northern Ireland*, © fpa.

Chapter Two: Abortion and Ethics

Abortion and religion, © Education for Choice, *A humanist discussion of abortion*, © British Humanist Association, *Hard questions*, © Life, *'It is very difficult to keep a 24-week baby alive'*, © Guardian Newspapers Ltd 2009, *Many born within abortion limit survive*, © Telegraph Group Ltd, London 2008, *Third of GPs 'would not offer abortion'*, © Christian Medical Fellowship, *GP abortion poll 'not representative'*, ©

Abortion Review, *Conscientious objection*, © Student BMJ, *Women want a stricter abortion law*, © Christian Institute, *Public support for early abortion laws*, © DWCA, *20 reasons to cut the abortion limit*, © The 20 Weeks Campaign, *24 reasons for 24 weeks*, © Pro Choice Forum, *Women perform 'DIY abortions' with online pills*, © Alive and Kicking, *Easy access to abortion makes sense*, © Guardian Newspapers Ltd 2008, *Teachers asked for advice about abortion*, © Abortion Review, *Shock tactics*, © Guardian Newspapers Ltd 2008.

Photographs

Flickr: page 16 (Steve Rhodes).
The Life Institute: page 31.
Stock Xchng: pages 9, 32 (sanja gjenero); 22 (Jeinny Solis S.); 27 (Felix atsoram, sasha dunaevski); 34 (Chris Greene).
Wikimedia Commons: page 5 (Klaus Hoffmeier).

Illustrations

Pages 1, 20, 35: Don Hatcher; pages 4, 26, 37: Simon Kneebone; pages 6, 24: Bev Aisbett; pages 10, 15, 33: Angelo Madrid.

And with thanks to the team: Mary Chapman, Sandra Dennis, Claire Owen and Jan Sunderland.

Lisa Firth
Cambridge
May, 2009